John Hedgecoe's
COMPLETE COURSE IN
PHOTOGRAPHING
CHILDREN

John Hedgecoe's
COMPLETE COURSE IN
PHOTOGRAPHING
CHILDREN

Simon and Schuster · New York

John Hedgecoe's Complete Course in
PHOTOGRAPHING CHILDREN
was edited and designed by
Mitchell Beazley Publishers Limited
Mill House, 87/89 Shaftesbury Avenue
London W1V 7AD
with Mel Petersen

Published in America by Simon and Schuster
A Division of Gulf & Western Corporation
Simon & Schuster Building
Rockefeller Center
1230 Avenue of the Americas
New York, New York 10020

Manufactured in the United States of America
1 2 3 4 5 6 7 8 9 10

Library of Congress Cataloging in Publication Data
Hedgecoe, John.
  John Hedgecoe's Complete course in photographing
children.

  1. Photography of children. I. Title.
II. Title: Complete course in photographing
children.
TR575.H34   778.9′25   80–5506
ISBN 0-671-41220-5

Contents

Introduction

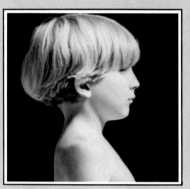

As subjects for photography, children are of universal and inexhaustible interest. Even when they are not our own, their spontaneity, energy and expressiveness make them subjects of unequalled appeal in many branches of photography, whether it is candid or studio work, portraiture or photojournalism.

In drawing up a plan for this book, I wanted the approach to the "how" and "why" of photographing children to combine teaching and demonstration from every helpful viewpoint. There are, therefore, five sections in which I cover every aspect of child photography. I begin with a short portfolio, in which I have aimed to convey my own fascination with and enjoyment in this field of photography. The following section, on appropriate cameras and equipment, puts in perspective the vast choice now available to amateurs and professionals.

In the first of the two principal sections of the book, Applying the photographer's skills, I deal with the basic elements of photography, such as handling shutter speed or depth of field, in the light of the special requirements of child photography. The teaching steps are backed up with photographs in color demonstrating the way I have applied the relevant skills in my own work.

The second main section, Analyzing the photographer's craft, takes as its theme a Photodiary covering the development of children from birth to adolescence. The photographs in color on this theme are supported by an analysis of the factors— sometimes compositional, sometimes technical—that I have borne in mind to achieve the results I wanted.

I have concluded my Master Class with a Photofeature which, I hope, will be an inspiration to students and aspiring professionals looking for projects of commercial value.

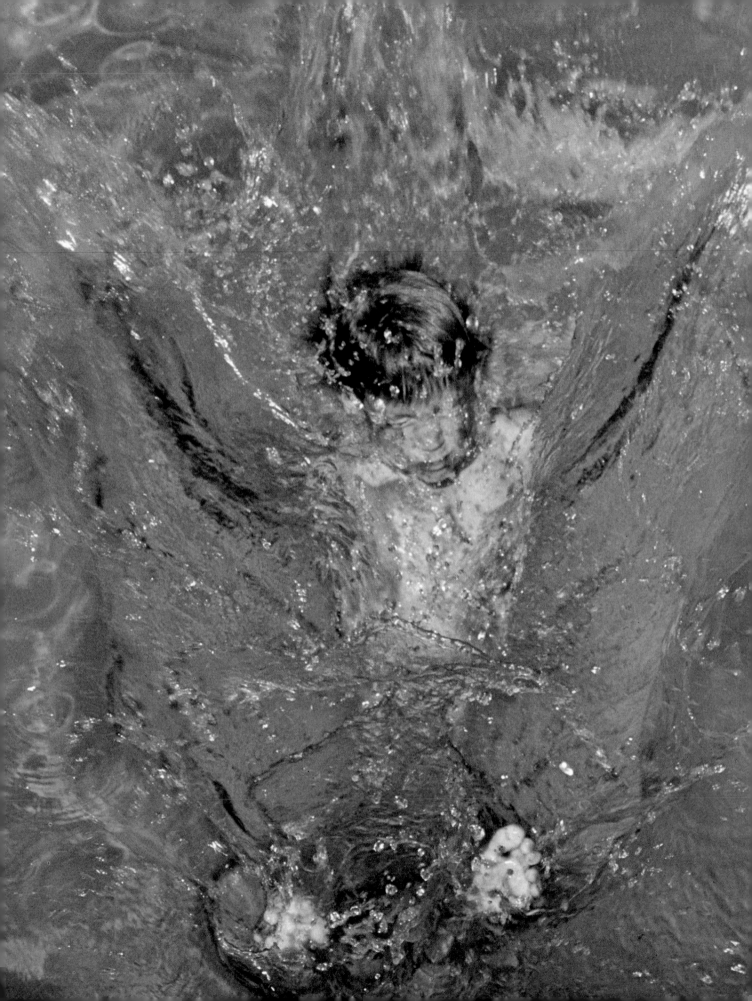

Pentax, 100 mm, 1/125, f4,
Kodachrome 64.
Dreams and reflections

Pentax, 50 mm, 1/1000, f16,
Ektachrome 200.
Making the big splash

Leicaflex, 135 mm, 1/500,
Ektachrome 400.
The party is over

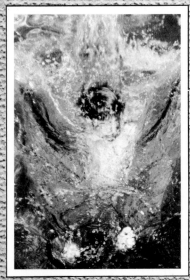

Pentax, 135 mm, 1/125, f8,
Kodachrome 64.
A decision of importance

Contax, 35 mm, 1/125, f8,
Ektachrome 64.
A sense of the order in things

Pentax, 100 mm, 1/60, f2.8,
Kodachrome 64.
Silhouetted figure in a circle

Pentax, 100 mm, 1/60, f2.8,
Kodachrome 64.
Gymnast – just holding on

Pentax, 100 mm, 1/30, f16,
Ektachrome 160 tungsten.
The observer observed

Choosing a camera

Of the many types of cameras available, the best all-round camera is the 35 mm single-lens reflex (SLR). Models available range from reasonably priced cameras with simple controls to expensive and highly sophisticated pieces of equipment, offering facilities which the beginner may not initially feel the need to use.

An SLR has many advantages. It enables you to maintain full control over focusing, aperture and shutter speed. Through the viewfinder you see exactly what the film will register when you actually take the picture. Light entering the lens is diverted to the viewfinder by a system of mirror and prism. Thus, when you vary the focusing and framing of the image you can watch it change in the viewfinder. Likewise, the depth of field can be seen and controlled.

Many SLR cameras have built-in light metering—sometimes known as through-the-lens metering (TTL). Advances in technology are largely directed at the SLR because of its deserved popularity, ensuring that it becomes increasingly sophisticated and remains competitively priced. It is also easy to handle and use—significant advantages under any circumstances but particularly so when fast-moving children are the chosen subjects.

Although supplied with a standard (50 or 55 mm) lens that is ideal for general photography, the SLR will accept a large variety of lenses and accessories, enabling you to build up a system of greater capacity. There are occasions when a standard lens can lead to frustration because the photographer cannot get close enough to capture interesting detail on a subject (for example, a child running about in the middle of a football field), or cannot get far enough away to include the whole scene (a view of the entire game). The addition of appropriate lenses—in this case a telephoto lens and a wide-angle lens—to your system will allow you to overcome most of these problems. The SLR has opened up the possibility of a total system—a single camera body which can be fitted with the appropriate attachments for photographing subjects as different as the moon and microscopic life.

There is a great variety of 35 mm film, designed to help the photographer operate successfully under the widest range of conditions. Film for 35 mm, whether used in an SLR or another type of camera, has a special virtue. The moderate negative size (24 × 36 mm) means that 36 or more exposures per roll can be provided. The camera does not need to be reloaded as frequently as others and wastage is not a major concern, encouraging the urge to experiment. This is the best way of improving camera skills and ability.

Larger rollfilm SLR cameras can also form the basis of highly advanced systems. The standard negative size is 6 cm (2¼ in) square, four times

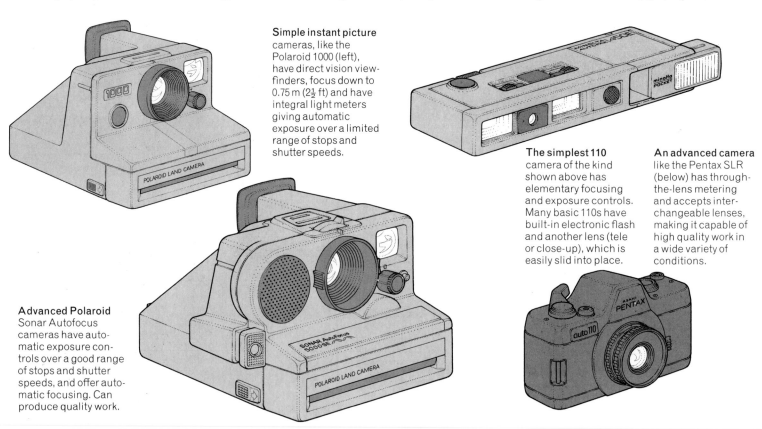

Simple instant picture cameras, like the Polaroid 1000 (left), have direct vision viewfinders, focus down to 0.75 m (2½ ft) and have integral light meters giving automatic exposure over a limited range of stops and shutter speeds.

The simplest 110 camera of the kind shown above has elementary focusing and exposure controls. Many basic 110s have built-in electronic flash and another lens (tele or close-up), which is easily slid into place.

An advanced camera like the Pentax SLR (below) has through-the-lens metering and accepts interchangeable lenses, making it capable of high quality work in a wide variety of conditions.

Advanced Polaroid Sonar Autofocus cameras have automatic exposure controls over a good range of stops and shutter speeds, and offer automatic focusing. Can produce quality work.

Most instant cameras now use dry-process film, where the negative is processed and a print produced within one piece of material— a white plastic card, which is ejected from the camera after each exposure. The image appears on one side, slowly reaching full density. It is then permanent. The maximum print size is 108 × 89 mm (4¼ × 3½ in).

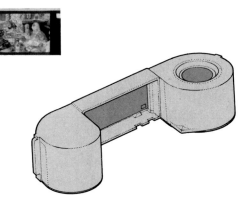

Easy-to-load cartridge film for 110 cameras has a negative size of 13 × 17 mm. This is too small to produce large blowup prints, though it produces quite satisfactory results up to postcard size. If 110 color transparencies are taken, they should be viewed on a special 110 projector, though it is possible to use a standard 35 mm projector.

larger than a 35 mm negative. Although a 35 mm negative can be enlarged to a great size, it must be of high technical quality to produce a good result. There comes a point where the larger negative will always give better image quality. Some 6 × 6 cm (2¼ in sq) SLR cameras offer the real advantage of an interchangeable back, which allows a different film to be used for alternate shots. These cameras are expensive in comparison with the 35 mm SLR and not so convenient to use.

A simpler 6 × 6 cm (2¼ in sq) camera is the TLR (twin-lens reflex). This has two lenses of identical focal length, one for viewing and one for forming the image on film. Focusing is convenient—the image which appears on the viewfinder screen is the same size as that which appears on the negative, but reversed left to right. TLR cameras permit the image to be seen through the viewfinder during the actual exposure. On an SLR camera the mirror flips up when the shutter is pressed to allow light to reach the film, and so the viewfinder is closed off and the image momentarily cannot be seen. On the other hand, the TLR is bulky and few models can accept interchangeable lenses. It is also subject to parallax error, because there is a slight difference in viewpoint between the top (viewing) lens and the lower (taking) lens, and this is noticeable in closeup work. Some TLR cameras have a parallax correction device built into the focusing screen.

There are plenty of compact, inexpensive direct vision 35 mm cameras on the market. They are generally equipped with simple controls—often with fully automatic light metering—which make them very easy to operate. They give a sharp, bright view of the subject and can be used without constant adjustment. Advanced direct vision cameras offer a rangefinder facility to ensure accurate focusing. Two images appear in the viewfinder. The focusing ring is turned until they coincide, and the camera is then perfectly focused. Some will take interchangeable lenses.

The 110 pocket camera is small enough to carry in a pocket or handbag and simple to use. In the most basic models there is no means of varying exposure or focusing; others are more versatile, having interchangeable lenses and automatically controlled exposure. Generally, though, the small negative size makes it hard to obtain good quality prints larger than 10 × 12.5 cm (4 × 5 in).

Instant cameras issue a finished, permanent print within seconds of exposure. The film is expensive but there are no processing costs, unless additional prints are required. The more expensive instant cameras incorporate focusing and aperture controls, allowing excellent results to be obtained even under difficult conditions. Professional photographers often use an advanced instant camera to check exposure before shooting a particular subject.

The non-reflex 35 mm camera (left) has an accurate rangefinder linked to the focusing ring. This is linked to the lens and shutter allowing manual adjustment of the aperture and shutter speed. The lens is not interchangeable.

The basic 6 × 6 cm (2¼ in sq) camera is the TLR (left) with an upper lens for viewing and lower for exposing. The more complex SLR type (below) accepts a full range of lenses and accessories. The folding hoods shade the viewfinder screens from extraneous light reflection.

A typical 35 mm SLR (right) will have auto/manual exposure control by TTL metering; shutter speeds that range from a second to 1/1000; a standard lens opening to f1.2, f1.4, f1.8 or f2 and will accept a variety of alternative lenses.

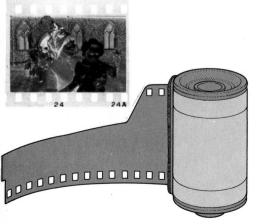

Cassettes for 35 mm film contain 20, 24 or 36 exposure lengths. The narrow leader strip is threaded into a slit in the camera's take-up spool and the perforations on both edges of the film engage on toothed sprockets which advance the film when the winder is operated. The film must always be wound back into the cassette after use.

Rollfilm for cameras taking 6 × 6 cm (2¼ in sq) format is paper-backed in 12- or 24-exposure lengths and the variety available is comparable to the 35 mm film range. It is loaded by threading a paper leader into a slot on the take-up spool. After full exposure, the film is sealed with gummed paper to prevent accidental fogging.

The controls of a camera

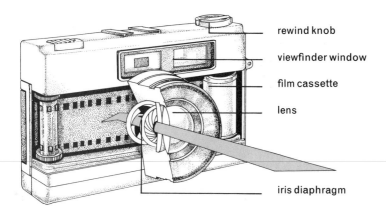

rewind knob

viewfinder window

film cassette

lens

iris diaphragm

This simple camera illustrates the basic principle of all photography. Light passes through a lens and strikes light-sensitive film, which reacts to the amount of light reaching it and records the image. If the film is to be exposed correctly, the amount of light passing through the lens must be exactly controlled.

When photographing children, it is often desirable to capture fleeting moments before they are lost. Being prepared is not a problem with simple cameras, where you load the film and are ready to shoot, and the many sophisticated automatic cameras now on the market. However, many excellent cameras are operated manually, requiring setting before taking an exposure. Many automatic cameras have override facilities for manual operation.

Familiarity with the controls ensures that no time is wasted when shooting. Set the camera for prevailing conditions. Adjustments may be needed from time to time, but making these should not result in missing the picture. The relationship of children to the activity that they are involved in,

Focusing on simple cameras may be fixed or limited to a number of fixed ranges. The SLR is focused by twisting a ring on the lens barrel. It is designed to be large enough to be manipulated easily while looking through the viewfinder. When the subject is sharp, the camera is focused correctly. SLRs are also fitted with a device which aids focusing by fragmenting an area in the center of the viewfinder when the lens is out of focus—useful for close-range work, where there is less room for error. Viewing is best carried out at full aperture for maximum clarity of view. The aperture is then stopped down prior to exposure. On many SLRs this function is automatic. The depth of field is the zone of acceptable sharpness extending in front of and behind the point of sharpest focus.

Most SLR cameras have the shutter speed control on top of the body, as shown left. The ASA setting is often incorporated into the shutter speed control. Many cameras have a "B" setting at which the shutter remains open for as long as the button is depressed, for time exposures. The "X" or arrow symbol provides synchronization for electronic flash. The bulb symbol shows the speed to use for bulb flash. The slowest shutter speed at which a non-professional can hand-hold a camera is 1/30—at slower speeds a tripod must be used to eliminate camera-shake, preferably in conjunction with a cable release to overcome the camera shake caused by pressing the release button. Even at speeds of 1/60 and 1/30, a firm grip and stance are essential to avoid movement.

Selective focusing can produce varying pictures from a similar viewpoint, allowing alternative emphasis to be placed on the same scene. Opening up the aperture reduces the depth of field and enables you to focus selectively. I took both photographs of the girls playing cricket at f2. In the top one I concentrated on the girl with the bat, picking a moment of maximum activity as the bat was lifted and her foot moved forward, her face showing fierce determination. The position of the ball reinforces the stress. The bowler's presence and contribution is recorded but not stressed. In the lower photograph the emphasis is reversed. Here the bowler, complete with ball, is the focus of attention and the girl with the bat becomes a passive element of the composition.

Movement can be communicated in different ways. In the upper photograph I set the shutter speed at 1/60. This was too slow to arrest the movement of the girl on the bicycle and consequently the image contains no detail. But the blurred effect heightens the feeling of speed while leaving the nature of the activity clear. You may choose to achieve an entirely different way of recording the same activity, as I did on the girl's return journey, selecting a shutter speed of 1/250 to freeze all movement. The result is this sharply-detailed composition with a pyramid effect. The sense of movement is communicated by the angle of the bicycle and by the whole pose—head down, muscles straining to propel the machine forward.

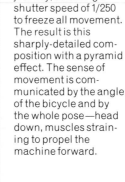

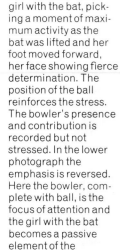

the resultant expressions, movements and attitudes must all be recorded in split seconds and such photographs should not be sacrificed in a last-minute attempt to adjust the controls more precisely.

First choose your film. The ASA, DIN or ISO number indicates the film speed—the higher the number, the faster the film. Adjust the film speed indicator on the camera to the appropriate figure. The exposure indicated by the meter will be governed by the film speed setting.

The camera has three main controls: aperture, shutter speed and focus. The aperture (f-stop) determines the amount of light let in by the iris or diaphragm. The shutter speed dictates how long the film is exposed to that light. Focus affects the degree of sharpness or blurring of objects in the photograph. Aperture and focus controls take the form of rotating rings set into the lens barrel; the shutter speed setting may also be on the lens mount but more usually on the camera body itself.

Most speed settings are marked in fractions of a second, from one second to 1/1000, with each progressive setting being twice as fast as the previous one. Aperture settings also follow a standard geometric scale from f1.2 to f22, and beyond; each increase of f-number halves the amount of light passing through the lens. The widest aperture (the one letting in most light) of a standard 50 mm may be f1.2, f1.8, f2 or f2.8 depending on make.

Correct exposure may be achieved through various combinations of aperture and speed setting: the faster the speed, the larger the aperture needed to let in the same amount of light, and vice versa. The two scales are directly related. If light conditions call for an exposure of 1/125 at f11, but a speed of twice that is needed to freeze a child in motion, constant exposure may be maintained by setting the speed to 1/250 and doubling the aperture to f8. Speed is doubled and so is aperture size.

To set the camera in preparation for a photographic session, set the shutter speed first—1/125 is suitable for stationary subjects, 1/250 if the subject is moving. Then take a light reading to establish the appropriate f-stop setting. Providing there is adequate light (if not, you will have to reduce the shutter speed) and you have selected a fast enough film, you can now focus and begin to shoot.

The aperture setting is closely related to depth of field, which is the distance at which a three-dimensional subject can be brought into acceptably sharp focus. If you focus on a child in the middle distance, and a house in the background is also in focus, the picture will have great depth of field. Most sophisticated cameras provide a depth-of-field scale on the lens barrel which relates depth of field, aperture setting and distance of subject. Some SLRs enable the depth of field to be studied in the viewfinder at the touch of a button. The depth of field increases with distance between camera and subject. As a general rule, greater depth of field can be achieved by stopping down the aperture and decreasing shutter speed.

Built-in electronic flash (left) is not a standard camera control, but it is increasingly available on sophisticated 110 and 35 mm viewfinder cameras, opening up new photographic possibilities indoors and out. Electronic flash is largely superseding flash bulbs—it casts better light and gives a large number of flashes before the batteries run down. Such units may have rechargeable batteries for use with a mains adaptor. However, built-in fixed flash has certain disadvantages. There is no way of "bouncing" the light to the subject, which eliminates harsh shadows, and the range and power of built-in flash rarely compares with that of detachable flash units. In color photographs, if subjects show red eyes it is because the flash has been too close to the lens-subject line.

The two cricketers posing by the tree show how the depth of field is altered by adjusting the aperture setting. The first picture, which I took with the aperture wide open, has a narrow depth of field and the result is that only the girl in the foreground is in sharp focus. By stopping down to f16, however, and adjusting the shutter speed so that the same amount of light is registered on the film, I recorded a much greater depth of field. The whole picture area, the background as well as the girls, is in sharp focus, and all details show up clearly in the photograph.

Automatic or meter-equipped cameras calculate exposure by averaging readings from highlight and shadow. This works well shooting with the light or in overcast conditions but, when faced with very bright highlights or shooting against strong light, underexposure will result. Some automatic cameras have a manual override to allow you to adjust for these conditions. In these two pictures, the girl was standing against a bright sky, the sun behind her. In the top photograph, exposed for the highlights, she has become completely silhouetted. If I had taken a reading from her face alone, the sky would have bleached out entirely. To fill in details of her face and keep the strong cloud shapes, I used daylight flash—on an automatic camera without manual override this would have been the only option open to me.

Light meters and flash equipment

Correct exposure is fundamental to photography. Unless you have a camera with fixed controls, some kind of light metering is essential. Advances in camera technology have resulted in increasing availability of cameras with built-in metering systems so that hand-held meters are now used mainly for specialized purposes.

Built-in metering comes in various forms. The simplest is a meter situated on the top of the camera which indicates the required aperture setting and shutter speed, which must then be set manually. In semi-automatic cameras the meter is coupled to exposure controls. The photographer sets either aperture or shutter speed and the other is set automatically. Alternatively, one control is set and a needle visible in the viewfinder moves as the other control is altered. When the needle is centered, the camera is correctly set. Fully automatic cameras calculate correct exposure and set the controls ready for use. In advanced cameras the chosen settings are displayed in the viewfinder. An override system allows the automatic camera to be set manually when required.

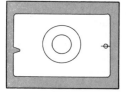

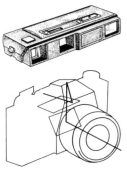

Some cameras—like the pocket-sized 110 shown here—are fully automatic. Exposure is calculated and controls set automatically, but there is no manual override. The SLR (left) is semi-automatic with through-the-lens metering. One control, in this case the shutter, is preset while the other, the diaphragm ring, is turned by hand until the needle in the viewfinder is centered in the circular mark indicating the correct exposure setting.

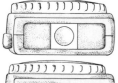

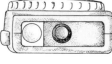

A quality hand-held exposure meter is often used by photographers who want maximum accuracy and it gives two types of reading. A reflected reading records the amount of light reflecting back from the subject. An incident light reading measures light falling on the subject. It is taken by sliding a diffuser cone over the cell, which is then pointed back at the light source. Incident readings are difficult with built-in meters.

Great care must be taken when shooting certain kinds of subject —especially with built-in meters. If a subject contains strong highlights and shadows, problems will be caused by the meter's response to the intense highlights. Meters cannot balance both extremes and come up with a correct median reading. In order to ensure that shadow and highlight are both properly represented when one outweighs the other, it is necessary to take two readings, one of the darkest significant shadow and one of the brightest significant highlight. If the two are averaged and the camera set accordingly, the result will be a more accurate reflection of the picture's tonal extremes. In the top photograph of the girl, the exposure was set for the brightest part of this high-contrast composition. As a result, a rather gloomy feel was created, with loss of detail in shadow areas. In the center photograph, the opposite effect was achieved by using a shadow reading, with consequent overexposure elsewhere. The bottom picture is the best, showing the combination of light and shadow that made the composition so effective. It was the result of a setting midway between highlight and shadow readings. Care must be taken when a subject is being taken against the light if detailing is required. If flash or a reflector are not available to lighten shadow areas and it is imperative that you shoot from that direction, expose for the shadow area only.

The use of additional artificial light extends the range of photographic possibilities. The most basic form is flash bulb, either in the form of single bulbs (used in a special holder) or the more modern flash cubes that fit directly onto the camera. Bulb flash is expensive because bulbs or cubes are discarded after one use.

Electronic flash gives repeated use from the same tube. Although initially more expensive than bulb flash, it is better value in the long term. It comes in various forms, from a unit that is fitted on the camera to large studio units used away from the camera. An alternative is tungsten studio lighting which has the advantages of low cost and the lighting effect can be fully observed before exposing.

Flash, on the other hand, has a particular virtue when photographing children. Their quick and often unexpected movements can spoil a picture, unless the camera is set at a high shutter speed. The high speed of the flash itself—between 1/750 and 1/2000 depending on make and size—acts as a shutter and arrests all movement.

Electronic flash comes in many forms. It may be built into a camera (top left) or detachable, as with the 110 (center left). A more powerful and versatile electronic unit (bottom left) prevents harsh shadows by bouncing light off its own reflector card. The tungsten lamp (center) is a typical studio lamp with a large reflector, giving soft, diffused light from a frosted bulb. To produce light of a similar quality, its electronic counterpart points into an umbrella reflector.

An eerie effect with the face highlighted dramatically was achieved by using a spotlight fitted with a conical "snoot" to direct the light beam onto a restricted area of the child's face. A similar effect could be achieved with an ordinary domestic reading lamp with a cone made of white card. I exposed for the highlights, resulting in a burning-out of detail in the face and the loss of almost all background detail. The dark clothing helps this effect.

Studio equipment

The photographer's workshop is the studio, designed to give complete control over lighting conditions and background for indoor photography. A studio can be anything from an empty room with white walls, natural light, camera and reflector to a complex place packed with sophisticated equipment. It is possible to create a simple studio at home, provided certain requirements can be met, which will increase opportunities for developing new skills and undertaking a variety of work.

There must be a good source of natural light (which can be closed off with blinds or shutters, permitting the use of artificial light during the day) and sufficient working space. A minimum of two meters (six feet) is required for background and backlighting behind the subject, and a similar distance between camera and subject. The shortest workable length of a studio is therefore four meters (twelve feet) though six meters (twenty feet) is ideal.

Walls and ceilings should be white, though one black or dark grey wall can be useful. Matt paint prevents unwanted reflection. The floor should be easy to clean to prevent a buildup of dust. If there is no suitable spare room, consider converting the garage—which can be modified more easily than a room in regular use. A drip tray under the car engine will stop the floor becoming oily.

Good natural light is essential. Its potential can be maximized by using a white or silver reflector card to throw light onto that side of the subject that would otherwise be in shadow. White walls achieve the same effect, while the black wall provides a dark background, preventing stray light from spoiling shadow effects. In addition to natural light, electronic flash (either fitted to the camera or as an independent unit), photoflood bulbs in domestic fittings and tungsten filament studio lamps may be used.

Other useful elements include a table for laying out props and equipment; good ventilation and heating; plenty of power points; dust-proof storage cupboards; folding screen; mirror for making up; stool and stepladder. The range of photographic equipment for studio use is large because you are not restricted by the need for portability or speed. The 35 mm camera has the advantage of being a good all-round system and the selection shown on the right contains all essential items for general use. Some professionals prefer bulky 12.5 × 10 cm (5 × 4 in) format cameras, which produce photographs of very high quality but have limited use in outdoor pictures. The 6 × 6 cm (2¼ in sq) twin-lens reflex cameras such as Rolleiflex are a good size for portraits and may also be used outdoors. The tripod should be used in conjunction with the cable-release to eliminate shake caused by pressing the exposure button.

For the 35 mm user, the initial choice of supplementary lenses is usually a 28 mm wide-angle and a medium telephoto lens. Although the latter conventionally has a focal length of 135 mm, the shorter 85 mm or 105 mm lens is better for studio work because it allows closer focusing. Using a 135 mm lens for a full-length portrait, it is necessary to stand over six meters (twenty feet) from the subject.

A studio need not be a complicated set-up. Even a spare room or garage can be used. Add an appropriate background by pinning paper or material to a wall or hanging paper in the form of a roller. Effective lighting can be achieved using natural light from a window and a reflector card (left).

Mother and child (right) were photographed in a home studio, where I used a bedspread as background to give the picture added interest.

Accessories for a 35 mm system

1 Sturdy tripod.
2 Gadget bag. Ideally one that can be used from the shoulder.
3 Camera clamp.
4 Camera case. Not used if camera is packed in gadget bag.
5 Spare film. Always take more than needed of transparency, color negative and black and white.
6 35 mm camera and standard lens.
7 Rigid lens case.
8 135 mm lens.
9 Gaffer (black) tape and masking tape.
10 Notebook and pen.
11 Cable release.
12 Lens hoods.
13 28 mm lens.
14 Lens caps.
15 Light meter.
16 Scissors and small screwdriver.
17 Dusting brush.
18 Clips.
19 Filters. Ultraviolet or 81A (preferably) and polarizing.
20 Portable reflector. Polystyrene ceiling tile or sheet of white card.
21 Neck strap.

Storage and presentation

A good storage system for photographic material is essential. The object is twofold—protection of work in good condition, and logical filing in a way that enables any given item to be retrieved efficiently.

Slides require particular care. They must be kept in a dry atmosphere in some form of dust-proof container. Avoid exposure to dampness or excessive heat. Normal room temperature is quite adequate for slide storage.

There are plenty of special-purpose storage aids available. Plastic viewpacks offer good protection, holding twenty slides in individual pockets. They are good for viewing a selection of transparencies simultaneously and may be stored in a deep filing drawer.

Special transparency boxes usually incorporate

an index card which corresponds with the numbered slots which hold the slides. If you have a magazine projector, slides can be stored in extra magazines. This is expensive and requires more storage space, but the material may be viewed immediately. Magazine storage is useful when the material falls into categories—for instance children at play, birthday parties or sporting events.

Negatives are best stored in strips, protected by special transparent or translucent bags. These may be kept in a negative cabinet with drawers, a filing cabinet or a loose-leaf album. A stationery ring-binder is ideal. Negatives are hard to judge at a glance—particularly those containing subtle detail—so it is sensible to make contact print sheets to be filed with the negatives for easy visual reference. Any prints that are not required for

display should be stored flat in a dry place.

It is important to label all material in some way. The information you choose to record should include a brief description of the people and the event, together with the date. This is especially relevant to photographs of children.

Mounted slides can be labelled with small adhesive labels. Colored stickers and self-adhesive numbers can identify categories or years. It is, of course, possible to write directly on cardboard slide mounts.

Negatives can be accompanied by technical information. Attach the contact sheet to one side of the negative bag with double-sided tape, leaving the other free for noting information in ball-point pen or grease pencil—though you must never write on a bag with negatives inside. I find that

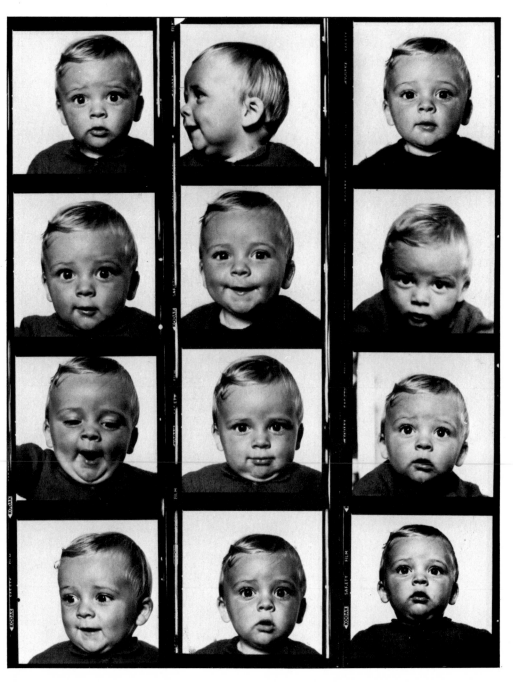

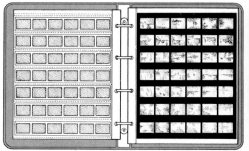

A **contact sheet** (left) makes it easier to evaluate the quality of negatives. Negatives and contacts may be stored together in a special filing binder (above).

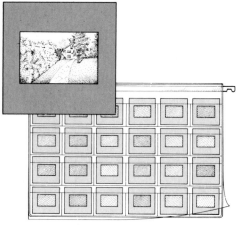

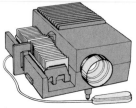

Viewpacks are ideal for storing slides. A number of slides may be viewed together without removing them, and the viewpack can be filed in a cabinet. Slides may be kept in spare projector magazines. This method—though expensive—means that material is always ready for viewing, and can be useful if it falls into natural categories such as annual vacations.

date, developer and film used is usually sufficient, though I sometimes add paper grade. If trying to perfect a particular technique, it can be useful to record additional information. The various results achieved by changing, say, the shutter speed and aperture can be analyzed and compared. The overall indexing system is a matter of common sense. There are many methods and you should devise one to suit your needs. The major consideration is ensuring that you can find what you're looking for fast, with minimal disruption.

Considering the effort that goes into the creation of good photographs, it makes sense to take similar pains with the presentation of your best work. Albums are the best way of displaying prints as a collection. A little imagination can lift your collection above the routine level of presenta-tion often seen in traditional family albums.

Avoid a regular arrangement of same-sized prints. Think of the album as a magazine and attempt to design the pages to achieve magazine-style impact, even to the extent of producing headlines with instant lettering. Create a photo-graphic diary—a visually-stimulating mixture of photographs and written commentary. With modern adhesives you can try alternative arrange-ments, lifting and repositioning prints until the desired result is attained.

For a more flexible—and decorative—display, a collage of child photographs mounted with pins on a cork notice-board can be effective, as can single montages of different prints. It is interesting, for example, to form a montage featuring a growing child over the years.

Dry-mounting is the best method for exhibit-ing prints, framed or otherwise, and is not com-plicated. Dry-mounting tissue, domestic iron and mounting board are required. Tack the shiny side of the tissue to the back of the print with the tip of a warm iron, not pressing too hard; trim tissue to size with scissors or trimming knife; place the print, tissue downwards, on pre-cut mounting board; cover surface of print with clean thick paper and, working with a medium-hot iron from the center out, keep it moving over print for thirty seconds, applying pressure. Add hardboard base, glass and clips for a print that is ready to hang.

I prefer to use grey card for mounting. This tones with the print and enhances the overall effect, while the more popular black or white can create unnecessary conflict.

Photomontage is an exciting technique that can produce excellent and original results. It involves the combina-tion of individual prints into a composite whole, and provides endless scope for creativity. There are certain basic rules to follow. I use prints on single-weight, matt paper for ease of cutting and retouching. Expressions should either harmonize or be in complete contrast for added effect. The originals should be lit in a similar way to ensure consistency of shadow and highlight. In the example shown, the portraits of the three children have been cut out and super-imposed on a base print of the family home. Before gluing the cut-outs in position I bevelled the cut edges with fine sandpaper and blacked the edges with pencil to disguise the join before pasting down. Once in place, the job was finished by retouching the boy's knee black and re-shooting the whole with a standard lens. Photomontage can be seen as a jigsaw puzzle in which you place the pieces where you like. Enlarge or reduce elements if you wish, or consider using the same subject several times. A child with varied expressions—or at different ages—can make an excellent and amusing montage.

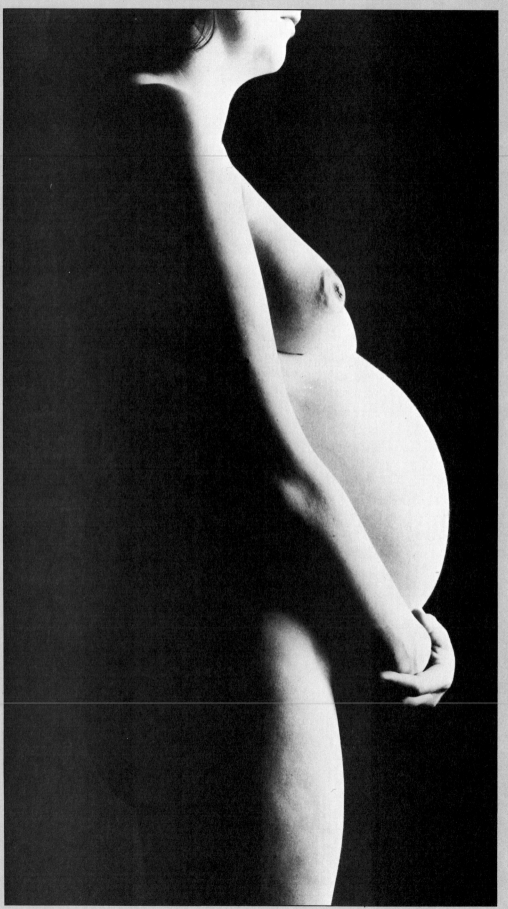
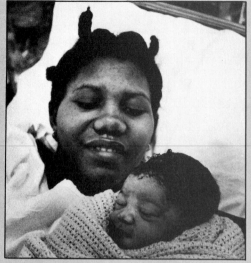

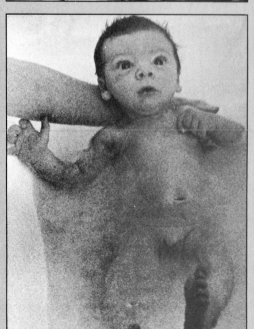

Applying the photographer's skills

Introduction

Mastery of the basic skills of the photographer does not involve a long and painful apprenticeship. Obviously, the more you practice and look at your results with a critical eye the more confidently you will handle your equipment and react to the photographic possibilities of a situation. What every photographer should be aiming for is an instinctive response to the exciting potential that children provide. The first essential, therefore, is to have the camera ready to hand and loaded.

Applying the photographer's skills to the subject of children requires as much understanding of the way they behave and react as of the techniques of photography. A little experience will quickly show you how the characteristics of children—their spontaneity, their vitality, their rapid changes of mood and their relatively short spans of interest—give wonderful opportunities for exciting photographs while compelling you to be adaptable in the way you go about taking photographs. Success does not necessarily depend on capturing dramatic or important moments but it does mean being ready to seize an expression or a gesture the moment it comes. There are few other fields of photography where you have to be as alert and attentive if you are to convey the essence of a moment.

In this section, I have covered the essential aspects of choosing exposure, depth of field, shutter speed and selecting film. I have also dealt with the way to use three different types of lenses: telephoto, wide-angle and zoom. Underlying this is my own preference for 35 mm single-lens reflex cameras that will take interchangeable lenses. Without being prohibitively expensive, they do provide the photographer with exceptionally versatile camera systems. However, my own preference should not discourage you if you want to spend less money on your equipment. Particularly for the beginner, it is a great mistake to be burdened with equipment you have not the confidence to use.

I have concluded this section by looking at the way the photographer works in different lighting conditions, including a simple studio. Studio lighting may sound forbiddingly professional but it is surprising how easily a temporary studio can be set up in the home.

Working out exposure

Choosing the right exposure is as much art as science, and no meter can tell the photographer what his choice should be. Nonetheless, the decision must be based on accurate knowledge of the brightness of the subject provided by a hand-held or built-in meter.

Often there is more contrast in a scene than your film can handle, and some part of the scene will then need to be under- or overexposed. One of the commonest pitfalls is presented by a bright sky behind the subject. The bright sky could mislead the meter into indicating a smaller exposure than is needed, and the figures would end up as silhouettes. On the other hand, children in sunlight seen against a deep shadow might be overexposed because the dark background dominates the meter's reading.

There are several ways to exclude a misleading background: you can move up close to the subject while you set the exposure, and then step back to take the shot; you can take the reading while pointing the camera at some other part of the scene that has the desired brightness (for example, you can exclude the sky by tilting the camera downwards, at the foreground, while setting the exposure); or you can take a reading from your own hand (assuming that flesh tones are the most important part of the subject, and that your hand is in similar lighting conditions).

It is important to know whether a built-in meter averages the brightness of all parts of the scene, or whether it is center-weighted—that is, whether the reading depends mainly on the brightness of the central part of the scene. Center-weighting is undoubtedly an advantage for rapid shooting, but a center-weighted meter must be used with care when the main subject is off center. It may be necessary to aim the camera at the subject to take the reading and then set the shutter before shifting the angle of view to take the picture.

A mother and her child make a delightful sequence of photographs shot within the limited environment of the home. Even in these conditions, the problems of arriving at a correct exposure vary considerably. By posing them in an exterior doorway (left) and exposing for the highlight, I have framed the figures and isolated them against the dark interior. In the same way, for the photograph of them playing together on a velvet-covered sofa, I have exposed for the highlight so that the complicated setting is in relative darkness. In order to convey the freshness of a sunlit room (opposite), I exposed for the shadow area and allowed highlights, such as the windows, to burn out. This element of overexposure has helped create the impression of airy spaciousness.

The area from which to take an exposure reading is that part of the scene on which you wish to concentrate—possibly quite a small part of the whole. In a picture of children outlined against the sky, for example, if you want to emphasize the detail of the clouds and reduce the figures to silhouettes, take a reading from the sky and expose for that. For detail in the figures, take a close-up reading from them and expose accordingly.

If, for a high-contrast scene such as a sunset, your meter gives an averaged reading, then the setting it indicates will overexpose the extremely light areas and underexpose the extremely dark areas. If you reduce the exposure by one or two stops from the indicated reading, there will be detail in the clouds and the landscape will be somber, creating a "midnight sun" effect. If you increase the exposure by a stop, the image of the sun will be burned out and the landscape will have a daytime look. This is a striking example of how exercising your judgement can create alternative but equally valid interpretations.

Errors in exposure may not be serious when you are using black and white film: a variation of plus or minus one stop may give an adequate negative. Color negative film must be more accurately exposed to about half a stop. In both cases, corrections for faulty exposure can be made at the printing stage. In fact, prints you send to ordinary commercial processors are automatically corrected to a small degree.

In the case of color transparencies, however, an error of one-half stop in exposure is the most that can be tolerated, and that only in special circumstances. If in doubt, experienced photographers usually bracket their exposure.

Diffused lighting (below) allows exposures that record a range of tones and subtleties of texture. *Rolleiflex, 1/125, f8, Tri-X.*

The dramatic silhouettes of father and son (right) were achieved by exposing for the sky. *Hasselblad, 80 mm, 1/500, f11, Tri-X, yellow filter.*

Contrast problems are accentuated when a bright light source such as a low sun (opposite) is included. Here, the lake provides fill-in light. *Hasselblad, 80 mm, 1/250, f8, Tri-X, yellow filter.*

Controlling depth of field

Controlling the aperture to change the depth of field adds a vital dimension to your photographs and is really as simple as it is important. The fundamental rule is, the smaller the aperture, the greater the depth of field, other things being equal. When focusing your camera by setting it against a fixed reference mark, you will notice that on each side of that mark is a series of calibration lines, each line corresponding to a certain aperture.

The f4 calibration line on one side marks the farthest distance at which subjects are sharply focused when the aperture is set at f4, while its counterpart on the other side indicates the minimum distance. Try varying the focus setting: the f4 calibrations indicate a smaller depth of field as you focus on closer images. So your focusing has to be more precise when you're shooting close-ups. Comparing scales on different types of lenses will show you that wide-angle (short-focal length) lenses have greater depth of field than standard lenses; telephoto (long focal length) lenses have a much shallower depth of field. To get the best out of different types of lenses, an understanding of these characteristics is as important as an appreciation of the angle of view.

You must be sufficiently familiar with the control of the depth of field to be able to make a conscious choice concerning it for every picture. Do you want as much as possible of the foreground and background in focus? This might be the case if you are photographing an extended group of subjects—some children near the camera, some farther from it—in order to make an interesting composition. In this case, set the smallest possible aperture. But remember that the shutter speed will need to be correspondingly slower, and if it is too slow you run the risk of blur due to camera shake or subject movement. On the other hand, you may wish to keep a distracting background or foreground out of focus in order to concentrate attention on the subject. Then you need the largest aperture possible, and a faster shutter speed to compensate.

Use the maximum depth of field when you want to be ready to shoot unpredictable subjects at a moment's notice. Choose the smallest aperture that conditions permit and set the infinity mark on the focusing ring just inside the upper marking corresponding to that aperture on the depth-of-field scale. Your depth of field will now extend from infinity down to some relatively close point, and only minor adjustments will be needed for all but very close subjects. With your camera set in this way you can photograph active children without having to adjust the focus for each shot.

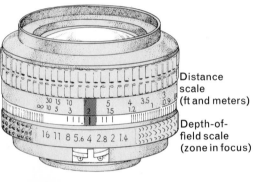

Distance scale (ft and meters)

Depth-of-field scale (zone in focus)

A standard lens for a 35 mm camera, set at an aperture of f4, shows the depth of field by calibrations that are read against the focusing ring. The zone of sharp focus decreases the closer the lens is focused. The depth of field is extended when the aperture is reduced from f4 to f16 (right).

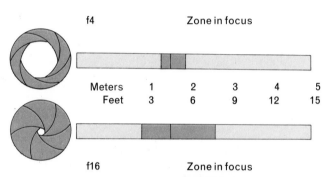

f4   Zone in focus

Meters   1   2   3   4   5
Feet   3   6   9   12   15

f16   Zone in focus

In these three pictures, for all of which I used a 35 mm camera fitted with a standard lens, depth of field has been used to enhance composition.

An open aperture of f2.8 allowed me to record the little boy (far left) so that he is clearly defined while the background is sufficiently diffused for it not to be distracting.

The silhouettes of two boys standing in a doorway (left) provide an unusual frame for a Thai palace. I stopped down to f22 to get an acceptable degree of sharpness over a maximum distance.

The bizarre pose of the smiling contortionist (right) is all the more striking because it is seen in conjunction with a boy standing normally. To concentrate attention on the girl, I used a wide aperture, exploiting the different definition of the two figures.

Though altering the aperture is a relatively simple technical adjustment, controlling the depth of field in this way is a crucial factor in getting the image you want. Varying the depth of field does not simply increase or decrease the area of image in sharp focus; it can modify the compositional, color, tonal and light values of a picture.

The effect of manipulating aperture is well demonstrated by this pair of photographs of Peruvian boys, shot through the open window of a stationary car on the outskirts of Cuzco. Both photographs were taken with high-speed film, which gives the additional flexibility particularly useful in conditions of mixed light and shade. In taking the photograph above, I followed the basic rule of shooting to capture the telling image without losing time on fine adjustments of settings. If you have time to take more photographs, then that is your opportunity to see how you might improve the image by, for instance, changing the depth of field. Though I wanted the solid presence of the boy in the black hat to be the dominant element, I felt it could be juxtaposed against the bright clothing of his friend. However, in this photograph I have used maximum depth of field so that the boy in the background in his multi-colored sweater overpowers the somber subtleties of the boy in the foreground.
Pentax, 50 mm, 1/125, f16, Ektachrome 400.

As the children were holding their pose, I quickly altered the aperture to f5.6 at 1/1000 second. This adjustment has considerably enhanced the composition and the aesthetic values of the picture. The reduction in the depth of field has resulted in the enlargement of the background figure, the softening of background color, the merging of highlight and shadow areas, and the toning down of all background detail. The boy in the foreground now looms out of the picture, indisputably the dominant element. The subdued background color intensifies the color of his clothing and, rather than being a distraction, the background figure has become an effective foil, though fully integrated with the foreground.

Selecting shutter speed

By using a fast shutter speed, 1/500 second or faster, it is possible to "freeze" the rapid movements of children playing. Slower shutter speeds may record the same activities with blur. Provided the use of blur is controlled, it can powerfully convey a sense of movement. Fast shutter speeds are, however, very useful if you want to record the highly energetic behavior of children. Fast film used in conjunction with fast shutter speeds allows you to stop down the aperture and record a reasonable depth of field.

In selecting the shutter speed for the effect you want, you must take into account distance from camera to subject and the direction of movement, as well as the speed at which the subject is travelling. A subject moving at a constant speed requires a faster shutter speed to "freeze" its movement the closer it is to the camera. As the table on page 39 shows, when a subject is moving at an oblique angle towards the camera, a faster shutter speed is needed to stop movement than when it is coming directly towards the camera. An even faster speed is needed to stop movement when the subject is travelling parallel to the plane of the camera.

Fast shutter speeds also help to eliminate camera shake, which probably spoils more pictures than any other factor. In unskilled hands, 1/125 second is probably the safest choice. With practice and in calm conditions, it is quite easy to produce second. But if you are badly balanced, or photographing in wind, use the highest possible speed consistent with available light.

Medium shutter speeds were used for the boy with the cat and the cartwheeling girl. The boy presented nothing problematic in terms of depth of field or movement and, by choosing 1/60, I was able to get enough depth of field to make both subjects sharp and to stop any movement likely to be made. I wanted to capture the girl's cartwheel at its climax in order to express the nature of the activity. I chose a speed of 1/125 because stopping the movement completely would have made the image look like a cut-out.

Slow shutter speeds were deliberately chosen for the girl playing blindman's bluff (below). I wanted to capture the instant when the girl was pausing, the static moment in a turbulent game. At 1/15, she is acceptably sharp, but the other children record as blurs. A faster speed would have frozen all movement but at the expense of atmosphere and immediacy. The boy being showered (right) was shot at 1/30 so the flow of water recorded as a continuous stream.

By **setting stopped action** against plain backgrounds, interesting shapes can be given strong emphasis. I was taken with the girl's ability (left) to jump high when skipping and with her beautiful, floating hair. I shot from a low angle to record her clearly against the sky. As I exposed at the jump's climax, 1/250 was enough to freeze most of the movement. To stop the movement of the little boy (below). I used a speed of 1/500.

Use the camera on a tripod if there is risk of camera shake— generally at any speed less than 1/60. If without a tripod, rest the camera, or brace yourself on something solid; squeeze the release gently.

Choosing the right shutter speed

Experience is the only way to judge accurately the shutter speed needed to stop an action, but the following table is a useful guide. Apparent speed changes not only with the direction in which the subject is moving, but with how far it is from the camera, and the type of lens in use. This table assumes that the subject is photographed in the middle distance with a standard lens.

Subject	Towards	Diagonally	Across
Portrait	1/60	—	—
Walking	1/30	1/60	1/125
Cycling	1/60	1/125	1/250
Swimming	1/250	1/500	1/1000
Running	1/500	1/1000	1/1000

Applying the photographer's skills/SELECTING SHUTTER SPEED

The energy and volatile moods of children make them endlessly fascinating subjects. Fast films and the fast lenses of modern cameras allow the photographer to pluck an instant from a fast-moving sequence and record it in crisp detail. However, there is no "right" shutter speed for a given situation. An image containing the blur of movement can convey the excitement and liveliness of children with more spontaneity and force than an image with all movement frozen.

Tantrums and tears are just as much a part of childhood as smiles and contentment. I wanted to convey the violence of this little girl's outburst, as she screamed and shook her head wildly from side to side. The camera was preset at a shutter speed of 1/250, clearly insufficient to freeze the movement but not so slow that the impassioned momentary rage records as a total blur. The result is a picture that successfully captures powerful emotion. *Pentax, 135 mm, 1/250, f8, Ektachrome 64.*

The whirling figure of the skateboarder was travelling at such speed that in the restricted area of the rink I could not follow him through with the camera. I wanted to arrest the movement so as to record the shape and form of the figure as it hurtled around the rim of the bowl. I pre-focused on a fixed position and used the fastest speed available. Fast film enabled me to close down the aperture and record a maximum depth of field. *Pentax, 50 mm, 1/1000, f16, Ektachrome 200.*

The choice of film

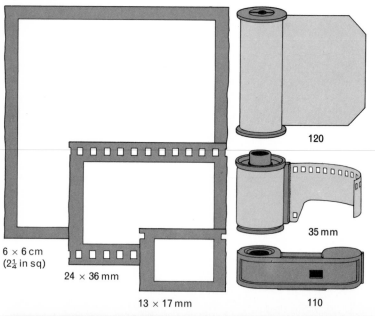

6 × 6 cm
(2¼ in sq)

24 × 36 mm

13 × 17 mm

120

35 mm

110

The sizes of film most used are 120 and 220 roll film, 35 mm cassettes and 110 cartridges. With 120 roll film there are 12 exposures and with 220 there are 24 exposures, both of 6 × 6 cm (2¼ in sq). Some cameras take 15 exposures on a 120 at 6 × 4.5 cm (2¼ × 1¾ in). Whereas 120 film has protective backing paper for its entire length, 220 has only a short trailer. Cassettes of 35 mm film come in 20, 24 and 36 exposures and are rewound before opening the camera. Drop-in cartridges of 110 in 12 or 20 exposures are not rewound.

The type of camera you own determines the size of film you use. The subject you wish to photograph, the lighting conditions, and whether you want to produce black and white prints, color prints or color slides determine the type of film you use. Black and white and color negative films produce negatives which have to be subsequently printed to give positive paper prints. With color transparency film there are no negatives; the final result is the actual film on which you made the exposure. Color prints can be made from color slides or transparencies, but the results are not as satisfactory as prints made from negatives. Color transparency films are available for daylight or artificial light and the correct film should be used for accurate color representation.

Films are also available in different speed ratings, which are measured in ASA or DIN. Both of these are gradually being replaced by ISO, a universally acceptable set of film-speed standards. For example, a film with a rating ASA 400/27 DIN will be expressed in the rating ISO 400/27°. Film speed is the sensitivity or speed with which a film

The face of a shy child holding her mother's hand provides a strong contrast to the white glove. The picture was taken on Plus-X film which has admirably represented the tonal range from black to white and the subtleties of texture in the child's clothing.

A sensitive portrait of this beautiful young girl is enhanced by the fine grained film in this picture. I used Panatomic-X which reproduced the even black of the background as well as the delicate textures of the girl's clothes and hair. The lighting was diffused daylight which also revealed the soft quality of her complexion.

An atmosphere of romance and mystery has been created by taking this photograph in the available light cast by a candle. Taken on a fast film (Tri-X), this picture has a coarse grain but also a high contrast because of the harsh lighting conditions. There is some loss of detail in the highlights and tone in the girl's face.

reacts to light. A film with a rating of 400 ASA is a fast film, and a film with a rating of 25 ASA is a slow film. Under identical lighting conditions a fast film requires a shorter exposure than a slow film to produce a similar result.

As a reminder of the type of film in your camera, it is always a good idea when loading, to tear off the end flap of the film carton and either slip it into the camera case, or tape it onto the camera back.

Normal film speeds, that is, the film speeds for average conditions, are 125 ASA for black and white, 100 ASA for color negative and 64 ASA for color transparency. Fast films are a valuable asset to the photographer, enabling pictures to be taken with available light where previously flash would have been necessary, but remember that a fast film may not always be the one you need. It is as much a disadvantage to try to photograph under very bright lighting conditions with a fast film as it is to try to photograph under very poor lighting conditions with a slow one.

Grain and contrast are also associated with film speed. The faster a film, the coarser the grain and the lower the contrast of the emulsion; there is, however, more exposure latitude with faster films. With fast color films there is also a loss of color accuracy, but grain can be used to good effect, and the color, although less accurate, is not unattractive.

Most color transparency films are balanced for exposure in average daylight and a yellow to amber overall cast will result when they are used with tungsten filament (domestic and photoflood) lamps. This can be corrected with the use of the appropriate bluish conversion filter; an 80A for domestic light and an 80B for photoflood lamps. Unfortunately, these filters also reduce the effective speed of the film by 2 and $1\frac{2}{3}$ stops respectively. A better solution is to use a type B film specifically designed for tungsten light, such as Ektachrome ET 160. Type B materials can also be exposed in daylight using an 85B amber filter with a speed loss of $\frac{2}{3}$ of a stop. This information is for producing color correct transparencies. Interesting special effects can be obtained by taking photographs in incorrect or mixed lighting. Fluorescent light is not suitable for color correct photography because it is deficient in certain wavelengths of light. Fairly satisfactory results can be obtained by using daylight film, although they tend to have a bluish-green bias.

Choosing a brand of film is largely a matter of convenience and personal preference because they are all of a high standard, but it is a good idea to experiment to find the ones you like and stick to them.

When buying film, always check the expiration date printed on the side of the carton so that you do not buy film with only a short life. When buying a quantity of color transparency films also look for the batch number and try to buy them all from the same batch. This is because the speed and color bias of color materials vary from batch to batch. With Ektachrome in particular you should note the instructions packed with each film in which the precise speed is given in red. In this way you will avoid having to alter your camera every time you change the film.

FILMS

Film name	ASA	Sizes
BLACK AND WHITE NEGATIVE FILMS		
Ilford		
Pan F	50	135-20, 135-36, 35 mm (reloads) bulk film, 120, 220
FP4	125	135-20, 135-36, 35 mm (reloads) bulk film, 120, 220
HP5	400	135-20, 135-36, 35 mm (reloads) bulk film, 120, 220
Kodak		
Panatomic-X	32	135-36, 35 mm (reloads) bulk film
Panatomic-X Professional	32	120
Plus-X Pan	125	135-20, 135-36, 35 mm (reloads) bulk film
Verichrome Pan	125	110-12, 126-12, 126-20, 35 mm (reloads) bulk film, 120
Tri-X Pan	400	135-20, 135-36, 35 mm (reloads) bulk film, 120
Royal-X Pan	1250	120
COLOR NEGATIVE FILMS		
Agfacolor CNS	80	126-12, 126-20, 135-12, 135-20, 135-36, 120
Agfacolor CN110	80	110-12, 110-20
Agfacolor CNS	400	110-12, 110-20, 135-24, 135-36
Fujicolor F-11	100	110-12, 110-24, 126-12, 126-24, 135-24, 135-36, 120
Fujicolor F-II 400	400	110-12, 110-24, 135-24, 135-36, 120
Kodacolor II	100	110-12, 110-20, 126-12, 126-20, 135-12, 135-24, 135-36, 120
Kodacolor 400	400	110-12, 110-24, 135-12, 135-24, 135-36, 120
Sakuracolor II	100	110-12, 110-24, 126-12, 126-20, 135-12, 135-24, 135-36, 120
Sakuracolor 400	400	110-12, 110-24, 135-24, 135-36, 120
COLOR TRANSPARENCY FILMS		
Agfacolor CT 18 (Daylight)	50	135-20, 135-36, 120
Agfachrome 50S (Daylight) 50L (Tungsten)	50	135-36, 120
Agfacolor CT110 (Daylight)	64	110-20
Agfacolor CT126 (Daylight)	64	126-20
Agfacolor CT21 (Daylight)	100	135-36
Agfachrome 100 Professional (Daylight)	100	135-36
Fujichrome RD100 (Daylight)	100	135-20, 135-36
Kodachrome 25 (Daylight)	25	135-20, 135-36
Kodachrome 64 (Daylight)	64	110-20, 126-20, 135-20, 135-36
Ektachrome 64 (Daylight)	64	110-20, 126-20, 135-20, 135-36, 120
Ektachrome 160 (Tungsten)	160	135-20, 135-36
Ektachrome 200 (Daylight)	200	135-20, 135-36
Ektachrome 200 Professional (Daylight)	200	120, 135-36
Ektachrome 400 (Daylight)	400	135-20, 135-36, 120

135 is the code for 35 mm film
135-36 reloads are lengths of film for reloadable 35 mm film cassettes

Film is by definition a sensitive material and it needs careful storage in a cool dry place. A refrigerator is ideal but take it out a full hour before opening the foil wrapping, otherwise condensation will occur. Films should be processed as soon as possible after exposure and kept cool and dry until that opportunity arises. Some films made for the amateur market, such as Kodachrome, are designed to survive various storage conditions before and after exposure without loss of color balance, whereas Ektachrome, primarily a professional film, is designed to be exposed and processed in a short space of time.

Commercial color processing is mostly automated and thus consistent but, because it aims only to produce a good average result from a good average light and exposure situation, it is often worth bracketing your exposure to be sure.

Although acceptable when processed commercially, black and white films are very easy to process yourself and the results can be much better. It also extends your control of the photograph from conception to final print.

The cool muted tones of a Peruvian girl in Lima (left) and the glowing, warm tones of a tanned sunbather (below) clearly illustrate the range of tones and colors modern color film can achieve. *(Left) Pentax, 100 mm, 1/250, f5.6, Kodachrome 64.*

The negative (left) is the final processing stage before printing onto paper (below). The colors are complementary; yellow appears where blue will be, magenta for green and cyan for red. *Pentax, 100 mm, 1/125, f8, Kodachrome 64.*

Working with a telephoto lens

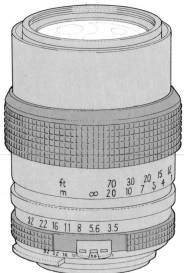

135 mm f3.5

Telephoto lenses are heavy. To avoid camera shake, use a tripod or, if the camera is hand-held, brace yourself firmly and support lens as well as camera body.

Telephoto lenses bring a distant subject closer by magnifying the image size. The longer the focal length, the narrower the field of view: a 50 mm lens gives an angle of view of 46°, a 135 mm one of 18°, while a 400 mm lens covers as little as 6°. Accordingly, as the focal length increases, less of the subject appears in the viewfinder.

Being able to stand at some distance from the subject while still filling the frame is obviously a great advantage if the subject is at all camera-shy. Many people, adults as well as children, are acutely conscious of a camera being aimed at them from close in, and this inhibits their behavior. With the photographer at a safe distance, they can relax, and better pictures will result. Candid shots, taken without the subject's knowledge, are also easier when working inconspicuously from a distance with a telephoto lens.

The visual properties of a telephoto lens make it a useful tool for photographing people. The most noticeable is the compression of space, which draws the background more closely in on the foreground and alters our perception of apparent space between objects. The longer the focal length, the more spectacular this effect becomes.

The limited depth of field of a telephoto lens enables the photographer, by judicious focusing, to blur out a distracting background. Using a 135 mm lens set, for example, at f4 and focused sharply on a child 3 m (10 ft) away, anything behind the child will be increasingly out of focus, and the main subject will stand out crisply against this blurred background. Details between the subject and the photographer will also be out of focus. Such elements can be deliberately introduced to give depth to the composition, or to add a splash of abstract color. This technique of differential focusing needs careful checking with the depth-of-field preview facility on the lens or by manually stopping down to the taking aperture.

Telephoto lenses come in a wide range of focal lengths, from about 85 mm to 1000 mm and beyond. A 2× tele-converter, an extra set of elements placed between camera and lens, is a useful accessory, effectively doubling the focal length but demanding extra exposure. Avoid cheap models, whose optical quality can be poor. The "portrait" lens of between 85 and 105 mm is a very useful one to work with: it enables the photographer to fill the frame for a head-and-shoulders shot without being uncomfortably close to his subject, does not distort facial features, and is not too strong a lens to use in the confined space of the average room. Outdoors, where distances are greater, the more powerful 135 mm comes into its own. In general, though, a lens with a focal length of more than 200 mm will be too strong to have more than a very limited application in child portraiture.

Telephoto lenses are longer and heavier than those of shorter focal length, and a faster minimum shutter speed has to be used to avoid camera shake. Though you can sometimes get away with slower speeds, try shooting with a hand-held 135 mm lens at no slower than 1/125 second, 1/250 second for a 200 mm, 1/500 second for a 500 mm, and so on. If conditions prevent this, brace yourself firmly against a wall or use a tripod and cable release—with the longest lenses this will be necessary in any case.

A Hebridean scene recorded with a normal lens (above) includes a lot of foreground. Using a 135 mm telephoto lens (right) allowed me to fill the frame with the main subject. At the same time, it has brought up the background, so that the image conveys the harsh isolation of this small group.

28 mm

50 mm

135 mm

The three frames indicate the areas of the picture that would be covered by three lenses of different focal length if the photographer remains in the same position. These three are applicable to 35 mm cameras but other cameras taking interchangeable lenses have comparable ranges. The photograph has been taken with a 28 mm wide-angle and the middle frame shows the area covered by a 50 mm lens, a standard lens for a 35 mm camera. The central frame picks out the area that would be covered by a 135 mm lens, that is a medium telephoto. The effect on depth of field and compression of space would be different with each lens.

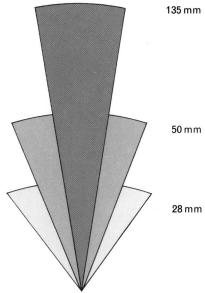

135 mm

50 mm

28 mm

The antics of a child showing off and trying to distract me needed to be photographed from a distance if I was not to shatter the boy's mood. Using a 135 mm lens enabled me to fill the frame with my subject and to capture the facial expression while having sufficient room to work.

The great advantage of telephoto lenses is that they allow the photographer to stand at a distance from his subject and yet record a sizeable image. Even a medium telephoto lens brings within the camera's capabilities a vast range of pictures which otherwise would be inaccessible. These lenses are particularly useful in photographing children, who easily become self-conscious when the camera is brought close in.

An intimate portrait of the girl and her pet rabbit was possible from a distance of about 10 yards using a fairly long telephoto lens. The limited depth of field has simplified both background and foreground, the shades of pastel green suggesting the atmosphere of a lush garden. *Leicaflex, 400 mm, 1/1000, f8, Ektachrome 200.*

A medium telephoto lens enabled me to capture the delight of this little girl and to isolate her and her shadow against the gentle wash of the sea. By taking up a vantage point on a beach and using a telephoto lens, it is possible to remain inconspicuous while recording the spontaneous play of children. *Pentax, 135 mm, 1/250, f8, Ektachrome 64.*

Using a wide-angle lens

28 mm

In comparison with standard lenses, wide-angle lenses have shorter focal lengths and take in a greater field of view. On a 35 mm camera, the focal length of a standard lens is usually 50 or 55 mm and its angle of view, about 50° or 45° respectively, is roughly equivalent to that of the human eye. Wide-angle lenses for 35 mm cameras are usually made in focal lengths of 35 mm, 28 mm, 24 mm, 21 mm, 18 mm, 15 mm and 8 mm or 6 mm, their angle of view ranging from 63° to 220°. The first three are the most commonly used, significantly increasing the angle of view in comparison with a standard lens without introducing an unacceptable degree of distortion. The last two are ultra-wide-angle or fisheye lenses with an angle of view of 180° or more. On a 6 × 6 cm (2¼ in sq) format camera, the standard lens usually has a

focal length of 80 mm and the medium wide-angle 50 or 55 mm, with shorter focal lengths available in certain cases.

Wide-angles come into their own when photographing landscapes or interiors and, more particularly, people or groups in their environments. Apart from simply getting more into the frame, the wide-angle makes these subjects look less cramped than a standard lens would and conveys the relationship of foreground to far distance, whereas the standard lens tends to relate middle distance to infinity. This is partly because the wide-angle covers not only the eye's main field of vision but also some of its peripheral vision—in other words what is "half" seen out of the corners of the eyes. People are often disappointed that some part of a scene that had a certain prominence when seen

The piper has been photographed with a wide-angle lens to convey his relationship, at a position in the middle distance, to the vast field of lush grass, emphasized by the inclusion of so much foreground.

The fighting boys occupy a dominant position in the fore-ground but the broad depth of field allows a striking contrast with a distant group of more orderly boys. With a standard lens, I would have had to stand further from the fighting boys to get them in the frame and the picture would have had less impact.

The cyclists preparing for a race were so hemmed in by the crowd that a wide-angle lens was needed to get these boys into the frame and all in focus. The dramatic angle of view has given a feeling of immediacy to this moment just before the race.

Distortion within acceptable limits can make a picture more forceful. A 28 mm lens used in this closeup of a girl at a party has exaggerated the size of the hand she is using to spoon food into her mouth. The distortion is not overdone but it is enough to suggest her hearty appetite.

with the eyes is either cut out entirely or appears insignificant in a photograph taken with a standard lens. The wide-angle goes some way to solving this problem—a particular advantage when foregrounds are concerned because they often have an important relationship with other parts of the picture.

The second key feature of the wide-angle is the greater depth of field it gives compared with a standard lens. At a given aperture and distance, a wide-angle lens will give far greater depth of field than will a 50 mm standard lens. This is an advantage when sharp focus is wanted over a long distance, but a drawback when selective focusing is needed.

A wide-angle lens also affects scale, making subjects in the foreground appear large compared with those in the middle or far distance. At its most marked, this becomes distortion. Although distortion can be used to create a certain atmosphere and, especially, a sense of immediacy when there are people or objects in the foreground, it is easily overdone and should be treated with respect.

Added control of perspective is given by using a wide-angle and this is useful when working in confined spaces: quite a small change in camera position produces a comparatively large change in viewpoint.

Some people find the choice between a 35 mm and a 28 mm wide-angle difficult to make. I prefer the 28 mm lens because, if used with discretion, most results are acceptably free of distortion and the wider angle of view does open up more possibilities. A 35 mm gives a "truer" result and for

this reason is preferred in photojournalism.

The ultra-wide-angles, otherwise called fisheyes, should be treated with caution: they distort all straight lines into curves, producing a round image. While this is a distinctive effect, it soon becomes boring if used too often. With a fisheye it is possible to achieve angles of view up to 220° but, because they need many more elements than a standard or long lens, good fisheyes are expensive.

Conventional wide-angles are compact and easy to hold and, although slower than standard lenses, are now being made with much wider maximum apertures than they used to be and can cope with most lighting conditions. Although more expensive than standard lenses, they are a vital acquisition for the photographer who wants to expand his capabilities.

Children's rooms, the territories that children consider their own, provide settings that express a great deal about character and interests. A wide-angle lens will be necessary unless you want to photograph just a small area. Using a standard lens in this study, the image includes only the boy at his desk and a limited background, which gives an impression of a neat, well-organized room. By using a wide-angle lens, I have recorded the whole room, enlarging foreground features and so emphasizing the characteristic muddle of a teenage boy.
Pentax, 28 mm, 1/60, f5.6, Ektachrome 200.

Close-up portraits with wide-angle lenses show a degree of distortion but, provided this is not excessive, it can help create interesting pictures. In this adult's-eye view of a child, the distortion has helped create an arresting image, the eyes at the center point providing a direct contact that offsets the exaggeration of the head. Choose the angle of view carefully and, for close-ups, limit the lens to a medium wide-angle: ultra-wide lenses give unacceptable distortion.
Pentax, 28 mm, 1/250, f5.6, Ektachrome 200.

The advantages of a zoom lens

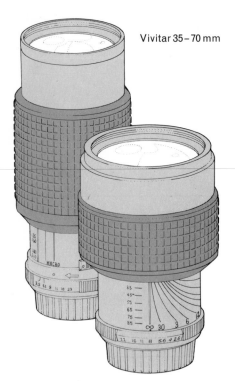

Vivitar 35–70 mm

Vivitar 70–210 mm

The major benefits of a zoom lens are the choice of focal lengths it offers and the ease and increased subtlety with which pictures can be framed in comparison with lenses of fixed focal length. A zoom does the job of two or more separate lenses, so you don't have to change lenses as often or carry so much equipment around. A 35–70 mm zoom lens extends the range of a normal (50 mm) lens to cover both moderate wide-angle and long lens work, while a 70–210 mm ranges from a "portrait" lens to a much more powerful telephoto with, of course, infinite variations within this range. They are more expensive than a conventional lens but cheaper by far than the three separate fixed focal length lenses whose basic functions they replace. Less time is lost changing lenses and many offer macro (close-focus) facilities.

The lens is focused in the normal way, and it will remain in focus no matter how the focal length is varied. Standing in a fixed position, the photographer can move in close to his subject by extending the lens towards its maximum focal length, or pull back for a wider shot, until the ideal composition presents itself. A zoom lens also enables him to maintain the image size of the subject as the child moves to and fro in front of the camera, though, as the subject-camera distance is now changing, refocusing will be necessary. On modern one-touch zooms this is simplified by combining the controls for focus and for focal length—the lens barrel is rotated to focus and

moved in or out to adjust focal length. Older models have separate rings for these functions, and two distinct movements are needed. With a zoom, there is thus no need for the photographer to dash back and forth following his subject—he can stand still and let the lens do the moving for him. Special effects are possible too: focus on a subject filling no more than half the frame and set the lens at the longest focal length. Then, while the shutter is open (a slow speed will be necessary), zoom back in to get a rushing effect of speed and movement. Experiment with different combinations of exposure and zoom as this is not the easiest technique to master.

Most good modern zoom lenses are of equal optical quality to fixed lenses, though this cannot be said of older or cheaper models. There are disadvantages, however. Zooms are more complex optically and there is thus more to go wrong as the lens elements loosen up with use. Their length and weight are greater than an equivalent fixed lens, so use a higher shutter speed or a tripod to avoid camera shake (test-exposing a few frames of film will soon show you the minimum speed at which you can *consistently* hold the camera steady). The maximum aperture is rarely less than around f4. Most fixed lenses go at least one stop beyond this, and so a zoom is more limited for low-light work. But for many photographic situations, particularly if only one lens is to be carried, the flexibility of the zoom lens far outweighs these disadvantages.

Taken with a 70-210 mm zoom at its shortest focal length from five yards, father and son are too small in the frame for any features to be revealed. The distracting background prevents a sympathetic composition without a different viewpoint.

By setting the zoom at a focal length of 150 mm I was able to cut out the background and close in on my subjects to show both their expressions and the subdued mood that characterized their relationship. All the important elements are retained.

For the third shot I used the zoom just short of its maximum focal length of 210 mm. The frame is filled with the heads of father and child. All distracting detail in the background has now been lost and attention is on their features.

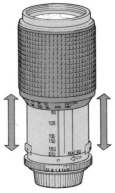

Zooming during exposure requires experience if you are to get a smooth movement in changing the focal length of the lens. In general, it is best to zoom at the slowest speed that is consistent with the amount of light, the speed of the film and your ability to hold the camera steady.

Trainee bullfighters in Lima, boys of sixteen, practice their elegant and dangerous passes with a skeletal wheeled "bull" before being tested in the real drama of the ring. There, the fate of the flesh-and-blood bull is certain but the vivid sequence of events culminating in its death is violently unpredictable. The *torero* tossed and downed by the bull was shaken but unhurt and recovered to deal the final blow.

The zoom lens was ideal for photographing the fast-moving sequences of these fights. My own position among the spectators did not allow me to move about so that with a lens of fixed focal length the size of the image in the frame would have changed constantly as the bull and the *toreros* moved backwards and forwards across the arena. By using a lens with an adjustable focal length I could keep the image at a relatively constant size as I photographed rapidly changing sequences.

Pentax, Vivitar 70-210 mm, Kodachrome 64.

Portraits in natural light

Natural light changes endlessly with location, time of day and variations of weather throughout the seasons. The photographer cannot control it in the way he can the lighting conditions in the studio but utilizing its varied range, from harsh glare to the subtle effects of soft directional light, is one of the most stimulating and exciting aspects of photography.

In child portraiture, the photographer aims to capture the characteristic physical appearance of his model while at the same time revealing personality and mood. If the portrait is of a group, the prime aim will be to capture the relationship between the members. Using bright natural light,

indoors or in the open, provides a good opportunity to capture individual expression and gesture, and the distinctive personality of a child or the character of a group. The photographer can often work informally and with great freedom while the subject is unaware of his presence. Even when they are aware of the camera, children will generally react naturally and without inhibitions to a sympathetic photographer.

The gentle diffused light of a slightly overcast day is particularly suitable for portraiture. It reveals a full range of tones and colors without creating harsh shadows. The photographer can move about his subject freely and shoot from

many angles while the model can be relaxed and does not have to squint into strong light.

Diffused lighting has the disadvantage of illuminating the subject and confusing detail without discrimination. Light-colored objects, in particular, can be distractingly conspicuous unless carefully integrated in the picture or eliminated by changing the angle of view.

Hard sunlight introduces problems of high contrast but it can create powerfully modelled images and allows the photographer to use shadow as a way of eliminating unwanted clutter. As other sections in this book demonstrate, all lighting conditions can be used to advantage.

Soft directional lighting, my favorite light for photographing people, allows the photographer and his subjects to move around freely without distracting shadows and sudden changes in exposure. It is ideal light for recording the tones in light clothing or detail in shadow as in the picture of the girls below, or the delicate skin tones of children, as of the little girl opposite.

The contrast of sunlit and shadow areas provides a useful way of manipulating the composition as well as conveying different impressions of children. When photographed in shadow area, the little girl with her arm in a cast did not convey my previous impression of pride in her injury and the background of shrubs and windows was distracting and complicated. I then brought her forward a few steps so that she was in bright sunshine. Despite having to look into strong light, she seems very pleased with herself and, because of the very contrasty light, the background has become simplified by recording as shadow.

Backlighting has helped portray the sunny and happy mood of the girls watching a puppet show at a party. The combination of direct and reflected light has produced an interesting range of tones from black to white. I have exposed to give detail in the shadow area of the foreground children.

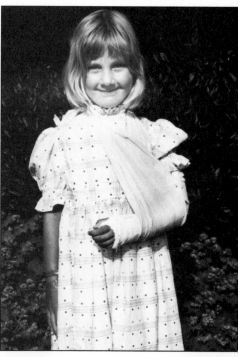

The transformations of color brought about by changing qualities of light can be used to strengthen the impact of a portrait or to give it a particular character. Even the high blue sensitivity of color film and the effects of colors cast by nearby objects and surfaces can be used to subtle effect.

Light in the doorway illuminates the figure but leaves the background sufficiently dark for the details not to be distracting. The blue cast has intensified the foreground color and has contributed, as has the slightly soft focus, to the evocative atmosphere. The striking appearance of the girl—with goggles, swimsuit in disarray, damp hair and whimsical expression —has made an unusual but authentic portrait. *Pentax, 50 mm, 1/30, f2.8, Kodachrome 64.*

Sunshine and shadow, only a few steps apart, have given strikingly different portraits of these boys. The change in the color of the light has transformed the atmosphere and mood. The predominantly bluish light in the shadow gives an impression of shivering cold. *Pentax, 50 mm, 1/125, f5.6, Kodachrome 64.*

Strong overhead light is usually considered not suitable for conventional portraits. Here it has created a warm and reassuring atmosphere and mysteriously masking shadows. *Pentax, 50 mm, 1/250, f8, Kodachrome 64.*

Mixed lighting conditions

Good photographs can be taken in poor lighting conditions where a satisfactory result would seem impossible without using flash. Light from a 100 watt bulb, candle or even a single match can provide sufficient illumination for taking color or black and white pictures. Indeed, the use of flash destroys the mood and feeling which are the essential strengths of such photographs, and creates an artificial atmosphere far removed from the original.

As well as allowing the photographer to capture realism and atmosphere, using existing light permits him to work more unobtrusively than would be possible with lamps or flash. Also there are situations where flash is unacceptable; babies, for example, can be alarmed by flash and young children rarely behave naturally when they are reminded of the photographer's presence by repeated flashes or over-bright artificial lighting.

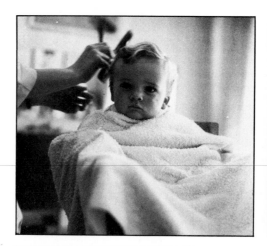

Using fast film and lenses at wide aperture (f1.2–f2.8) in conjunction with slow shutter speeds makes it possible to work successfully under bad existing light conditions, although viewpoint and camera angle may be restricted. A mixture of natural light and weak artificial light can produce interesting color results. The choice of film will also affect the color balance of a photograph. Usually, the light that predominates should dictate the film you use but beautiful and dramatic effects can be produced by using, say, a tungsten film at sunset, which will turn reddish skies magenta.

Photograph with light from behind the camera illuminating the subject where possible, taking care not to mask the source. Evaluate the existing light and select a viewpoint, positioning the subject to take maximum advantage of the best-lit area. Look for such natural reflectors as light-colored walls to reduce contrast, or use a white card reflector. People sitting or leaning against a wall can usually hold still for up to half a second.

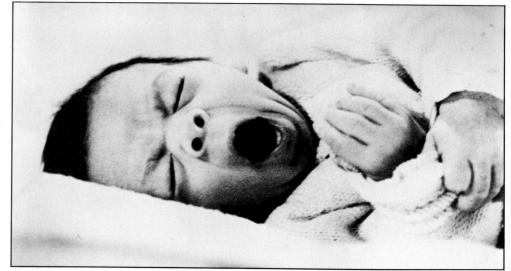

Since slow shutter speeds are usually required under adverse lighting conditions, a tripod to eliminate camera shake is advantageous where circumstances permit its use. Otherwise the camera may be steadied by adopting a braced position against a wall, a table or a friend's back.

A sensitive light meter is helpful; the CdS type is preferable to the selenium meter, which reacts more slowly. Expose for medium shadow area where there is a single weak light source like 100 watt bulbs or oil lamps. The excessive contrast caused by localized areas of bright light can be turned to advantage, providing deliberately dramatic effects.

In poor light where detail is limited, the pose adopted by the subject should reveal some of that person's characteristics. Film cannot always record details you can see with your eye; for example, a room lit by the soft glow of a single lamp may look attractive but contrast will be so great that extra exposure for details will be required, which will also burn out excessive highlights. In minimal light, try uprating a fast film from, say, 400 ASA to 1200 ASA. This works best in soft, diffused light. Development time is increased correspondingly—cut off the first few frames and develop them first, adjusting the time for the remaining film according to the result.

The first haircut (far left) is worth recording. The site is well lit, posing few exposure problems. I shot against the light, exposing for the shadowed face to capture the boy's expression.

For the picture (left) I insisted the sparkler be held at arm's length since fireworks are dangerous and extreme care must be taken when using them to create atmospheric pictures. The boy's sister held the sparkler in the foreground. I used Ilford HP4 film and 1/30 at f5.6 here.

Bright hospital lights enabled me to photograph the newborn baby (center) at 1/125 and f4 on a 100 mm lens using fast film.

The depressing atmosphere of this hospital waiting room (bottom) would have been lost with flash, so I used a fast film and a slow shutter speed made possible by the stillness of the subjects. Lighting was a standard bulb—the arc it throws stresses the relationship of the mother and her sick child as he burrows for comfort into her protective arms.

The district nurse (right) is a vital part of rural life, sweeping in to take control at times of need. She bathed and changed this baby and was on her way again in ten minutes. I used 1250 ASA film at 1/125 and f4 under a 100 watt light. The background bleached out but I was more interested in the commanding eyes of the nurse and the secure contentment of the baby nestling against her ample bosom.

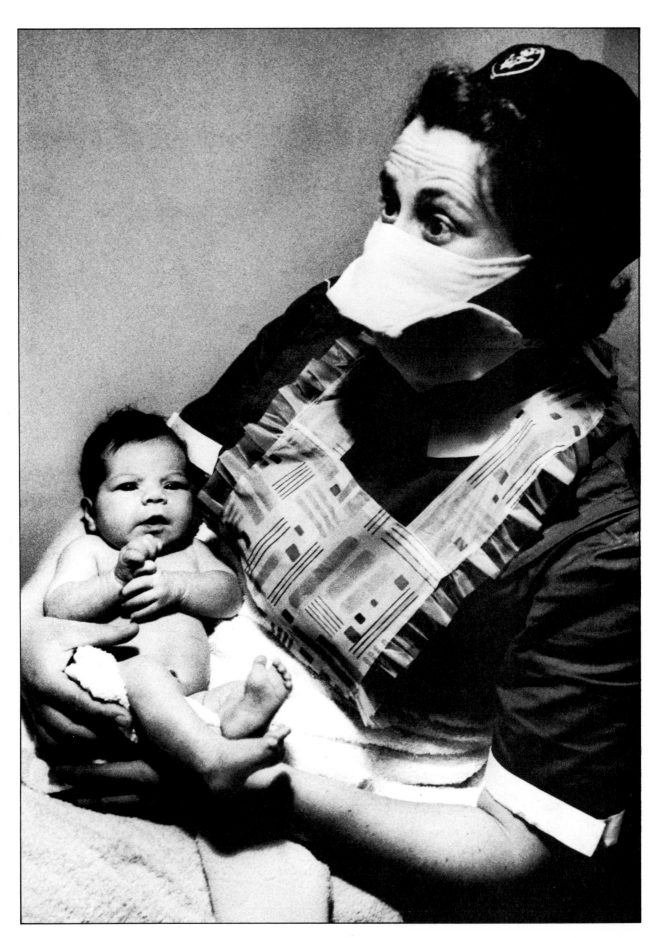

Modern cameras and fast films now make it possible to take black and white or color photographs in light conditions that, until recently, would have defeated all but professionals.

By using existing light, the photographer can remain an inconspicuous observer, free to capture atmosphere and unselfconscious expression. Even the deterioration of color in weak light or a color cast can contribute to a truer and more interesting image than that created by additional lighting, which would show color as if seen in daylight.

In mixed lighting conditions, the choice of color film is normally determined by the kind of light that predominates: daylight film when daylight is the principal source of light, and tungsten film when artificial light predominates. The photographs below and on the opposite page were both taken, using daylight film, in a Portuguese restaurant. In that below, the proprietor's daughter has been caught reacting to her father's banter just as an outside door is opened letting daylight illuminate her face.

Composition and lighting focus attention on her mouth, which expresses so much life.
Pentax, 135 mm, 1/125, f3.5, Ektachrome 400.

The daylight fluorescent tube provides the main source of illumination in the picture opposite. Though including the light has made it a powerful element in the picture, attention is held down by the strong yellow of the ashtray and the intensity of the girl's eyes.
Pentax, 50 mm, 1/30, f2, Ektachrome 400.

Studio lighting techniques

Photoflood tungsten lights arranged in a group can be used as the source of your "key" light. A screen of translucent white paper or cloth diffuses and softens the light.

An improvised studio provides controlled lighting conditions that greatly extend the photographer's scope. Children find a photographic session in a studio great fun but it is essential to have your lighting and equipment set up in advance as children soon become distracted or bored if they are kept waiting.

It is important to be able to experiment, so your lighting should be as easy as possible to vary. For most photographs, you will not need more than two lighting units. One will provide your main or "key" light, while the other, positioned on the other side of the subject, will provide "fill-in" light. Ideally, both lighting units should be mounted on lightweight, movable stands that are adjustable for height.

Tungsten lamps have the great advantage that you can see the lighting effect on the model while composing the picture and you can make exposure measurements with an ordinary light meter. But lamps are expensive and can distract your subjects with the glare and heat they produce. They also require relatively long exposures. Flash units are less obtrusive and their light is the same color as daylight. Flash is also useful as a fill-in light source when existing light conditions are contrasty. However, it requires experience to judge the lighting effect they create. The required exposure can also be difficult to calculate when more than one flash is used, and you may need to buy a special flash meter.

The most useful type of reflector bowl is broad and shallow, providing a diffuse light. The light can be further softened by screening it with translucent paper on a white sheet or by bouncing it off a flat white reflector of cardboard, polystyrene, or crumpled aluminum foil. A white or grey wall or ceiling makes a useful reflector. Colored surfaces, even furnishings, can produce color casts. When you use the daylight available in your studio, you may need to soften it by pinning thin white paper or a sheet over the window. It is useful, too, if you are able to black out the studio completely because you can control the lighting effects more easily.

Usually there is enough "spill" available from your light sources to illuminate the background sufficiently, but remember that any unevenness in its brightness will be exaggerated by your film and may spoil the picture. A plain, light background with almost shadowless lighting creates a brightness of mood well suited to child portraits.

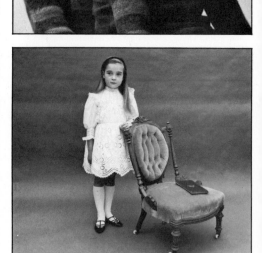

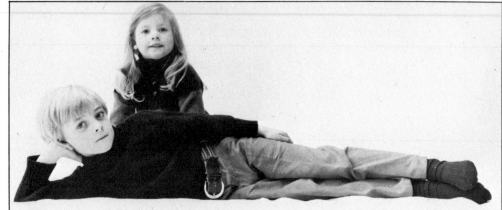

Sitting for a formal portrait should never become a forbidding and daunting experience for your subjects. By establishing a relaxed atmosphere, I soon found this brother and sister suggesting different ways in which they could arrange themselves. A plain background and diffused lighting have enabled me to take advantage of their inventiveness and pleasure in what for them became a game.

Eliciting a natural response is an important part of the photographer's task when taking portraits in the studio. Your own confidence and a sympathetic attitude will make it easy for a subject to react without inhibition. Use a cable release and talk to your subject while you are taking an exposure. In portraying this teenage girl, I have taken care to show adequate modelling in her face and hair.

Dressing up and careful grooming create a sense of occasion to which many children react very positively. This little girl was full of poise and confidence so that I felt it was best to make the most of the period flavor in her dress and hair style. A chair provides a useful prop even when your subject is not seated. To soften the formality of these pictures I have experimented with a relatively high angle of view.

A casual pose can be just as attractive in a studio shot as in a candid shot outdoors. These two children were intrigued by the photographer getting down to floor level. They have made a strong triangular shape that shows up forcefully against a plain background.

Young children quickly lose their self-consciousness if given something to play with or some activity to be involved in. Lightweight boxes provided the materials for a building game that kept this little girl amused during many sequences of construction and demolition. A series of photographs treated as a montage makes an attractive alternative to a single shot.

Portraits are among the first photographs anyone takes. Family, relatives and friends are, after all, the most accessible and obliging subjects for candid photography. Formal portraiture involves an element of conscious posing but the same subjects are an ideal starting point. Despite the way it is described, a formal sitting should not be a staid and unexciting activity. If it is, there is a very good chance that the photographer will fail to gain the confidence of his sitter and without that there is little likelihood that the final result will be a sympathetic portrait. Particularly for photographs of children, using the home rather than the studio allows the photographer to establish an easy and relaxed atmosphere.

Family groups, as the one photographed here, offer intriguing possibilities for single portraits and for various combinations of family members. On this occasion, I chose to photograph in the family's own home, using a minimum of equipment: a camera fitted with a cable release and mounted on a tripod, and one flashlight fitted with a reflector as the only light source. I started with the whole family, and quickly established a relaxed mood. It is sometimes useful with a group such as this to break the ice by telling them a story or getting them to sing. In trying various combinations of the children, I was attracted by the idea of using the double chair as a central prop and built up a pattern of faces based on the twin sisters. Even with a group of this size, there is an enormous range of variations open to the photographer. While I wanted to convey the feeling of family in the group photographs, in the individual portraits I have exploited personal features—pretty hair, attractive hands and elegant profiles—and used furniture as props where it has helped the subject to pose.

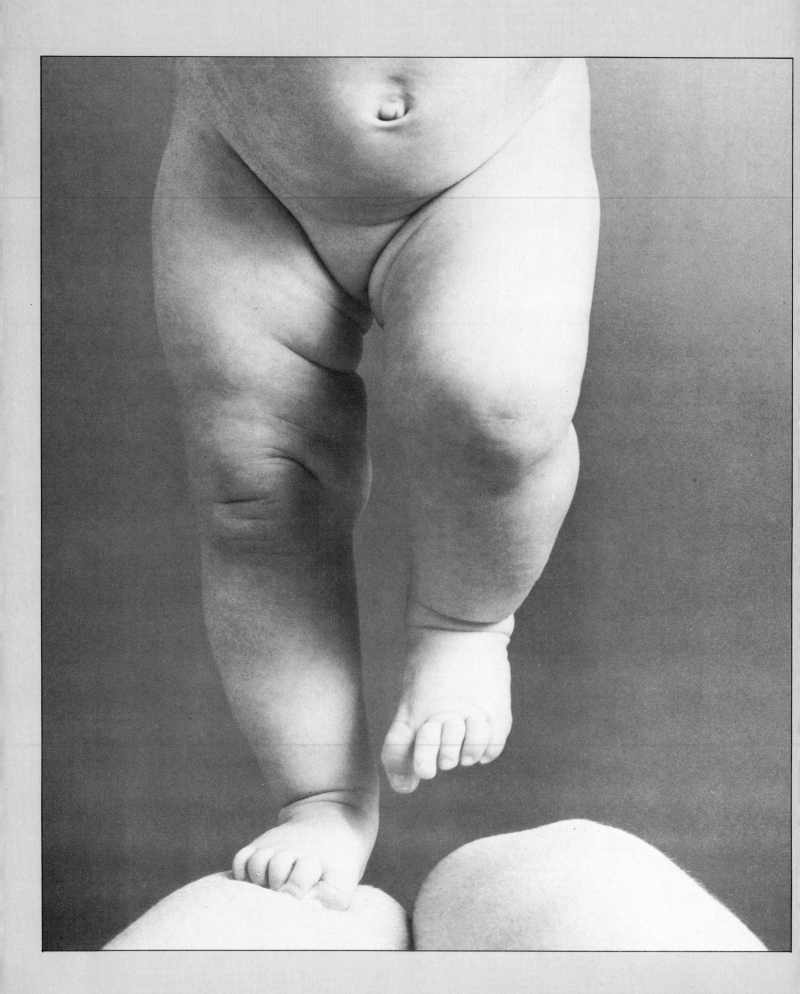

Analyzing the photographer's craft

Introduction

To capture the stages in the development of children from birth to adolescence is one of the most exciting and rewarding projects the photographer can undertake. I have chosen it as the theme for the analysis section of this book not only because of its intrinsic interest but also because it is a photographic project many parents begin with on the arrival of their first child. Your own family probably provides the material of the most absorbing and consistent interest. The pity is that so many projects are not carried through. I hope that my Photodiary will encourage you to sustain a project through to the point when your own children are grown up and that with guidance on the aesthetic and technical aspects you can turn your family album into an original portfolio.

I have not, however, thought exclusively in terms of the family photographer. My own Photodiary is not limited to a single family. Instead, I have aimed to convey the stages of growing up as they are experienced and observed in many different countries. Photographs of children, as photographs of any other subject, should and can have an interest that goes beyond our personal attachment to the subjects portrayed. One of the particularly attractive aspects of photographing children is that, despite vast differences of background, their expressions and gestures reveal our common humanity.

In the analysis pages, I look at the major compositional factors in photography: choosing the angle of view, exploiting shape and form, framing the picture, using tone and color in composition and relating subject to background, all contributions to the success of a picture. I also look at the application of specialized techniques, such as panning to convey movement and daylight flash to freeze movement. I have also included other pages of analysis that lay the emphasis where I believe it properly belongs, that is, on the need to exploit the photographic potential of every situation, even if it means ignoring compositional and technical perfection. When photographing children, the first aim should always be to capture the characteristic but often fleeting expressions, moods and activities of children, wherever they may be.

Babies and young children are highly unpredictable subjects. Photographing them successfully requires as much patience, gentleness and understanding of children as it does knowledge of photographic techniques. Good results are most easily achieved when babies are in warm, calm and familiar surroundings with mother close to hand. Even in these conditions, a photographic session should not last more than fifteen minutes. Frequent short sessions are much more productive than one that is long drawn out. A well-lit position with uncomplicated background avoids the use of flash, which can be disturbing to very young children, and provides a setting without distracting detail. By pre-setting the camera, the photographer can concentrate on capturing expression and gesture. When young babies are to be photographed lying down, it is useful to fix the camera on a tripod and to focus and frame so that there is an allowance for slight movement of the subject. Then, instead of peering through the viewfinder, the photographer can look directly at the child, communicating with him in a normal manner, and take photographs at the appropriate moment by means of a cable release.

A series of profile photographs taken over a period of months or years provides an interesting portfolio of pictures documenting development from babyhood to childhood.
Pentax, 50 mm, 1/125, f8, Ektachrome 200.

By taking a simple approach to camera angle, background and lighting, the photographer can concentrate totally on shape and expression. Note that the creased blanket helps convey a feeling of warmth and movement.
Pentax, 50 mm, 1/125, f8, Ektachrome 200.

The anxious child is generally more cooperative in the safety of his mother's arms. The relationship of mother and child is strongly evident in this picture, but positioning the mother in shadow has given greater emphasis to the child.
Pentax, 50 mm, 1/125, f5.6, Ektachrome 200.

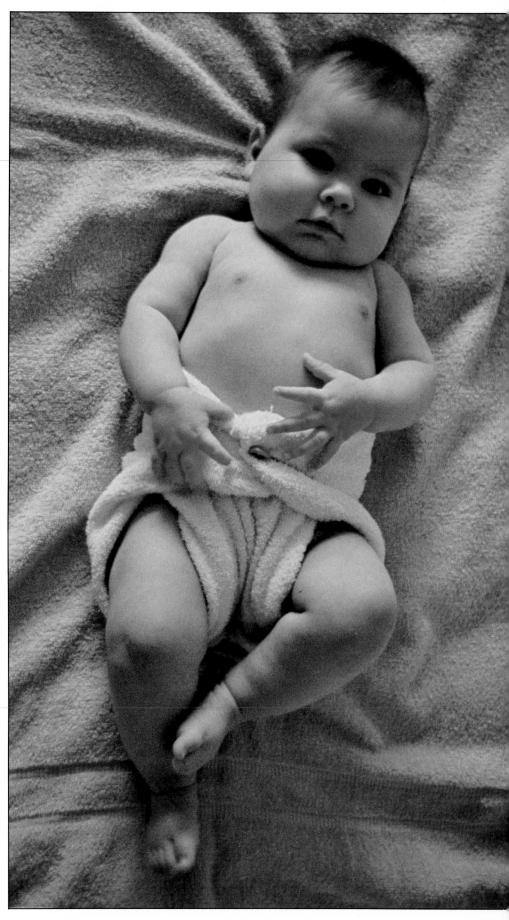

Analyzing the photographer's craft

Varying the angle of view

By experimenting with the angle of view, the photographer can make the most of existing lighting conditions as well as controlling the composition and the way children are shown in relation to their surroundings.

Parents photographing the family, just as much as professionals undertaking commissions, want their photographs of children to be interesting and varied. One of the most neglected ways of giving photographs variety—and one of the easiest to achieve—is to change the angle of view.

The inexperienced photographer tends to allow the camera and his own habits of posture to dictate the angle at which he photographs his subject. Armed with a single-lens reflex, he holds the camera at eye level and shoots down from a standing position. Such a viewpoint may produce very attractive results for some shots, but can often ruin others. Getting an interesting angle on children may mean crouching, sitting, lying on the ground, or standing on a chair while at the same time directing the camera upwards, downwards, to the left, to the right, or straight ahead.

Changing the angle of view not only enables the photographer to see children with a fresh eye and to capture the whole range of their activities and expression, but it also gives an important degree of flexibility in composing a picture. A relatively slight alteration of the angle may produce a very marked difference. For instance, it can transform a picture containing distracting detail and a cluttered background into one in which the subject, whether an individual or a group, is presented either in perfect harmony with its background or, alternatively, effectively isolated from it.

An interesting album includes pictures taken from many angles. The relatively flat angle used to photograph the boy on a beach (top left) has related him to a vast expanse of deserted sand. By taking from a higher level and looking down (top right), I have concentrated on the boy's shape and movement. In contrast to both of these photographs, the baby sitting on a beach (middle left) has been taken, using a Rolleiflex, at his own level. In capturing the child's pleasure at its first attempts to stand up (center right), I have used a steep angle to contrast the light tones of the child with the dark background. Sometimes, however, it is impossible to eliminate all distracting detail. In photographing the girl in her classroom (bottom left), I used an angle that minimizes detail but suggests the setting. The controlled lighting conditions of the studio (bottom right) gave me the freedom to explore many angles and to wait for the right expression. When photographing a series, it is an advantage to have a single angle view and a plain background. For the photographs opposite I sat on a pair of steps in a well-lit, well-heated room and concentrated on capturing interesting shapes and expressions resulting when a contented baby was left to itself.

The appealing shapes and forms of children—delicate and vulnerable, or firm and robust—can say a great deal about their personalities. However, it is important to avoid striving so hard for compositional effect that the spontaneity and freshness of a child's behavior or expression are destroyed.

Babies' clothing, which is often light in color, is easily overexposed if photographed in bright light. Overexposure burns out the detail and destroys all the indicators of form, simply leaving the shape or outline. To capture the delicate tonal range and so fill in the form of the curious doll-like child photographed in a Peruvian village, I photographed in soft, shaded light, taking a reading from the child's clothes.
Pentax, 50 mm, 1/125, f8, Ektachrome 400.

The concentration of the little girl was captured using a medium-length tele-photo lens. Despite the unselfconsciousness of the subject, the picture contains elements of careful composition. The chair, clearly contained within a space, provides a frame for the child. Hat and chair are strongly related in shape, texture and color and the daisy in her hand is a link with the flowered grass. The smooth body of the child and the delicacy of her form revealed in the weak evening light are subtly contrasted against the latticework of the chair.
Pentax, 135 mm, 1/125, f8, Ektachrome 64.

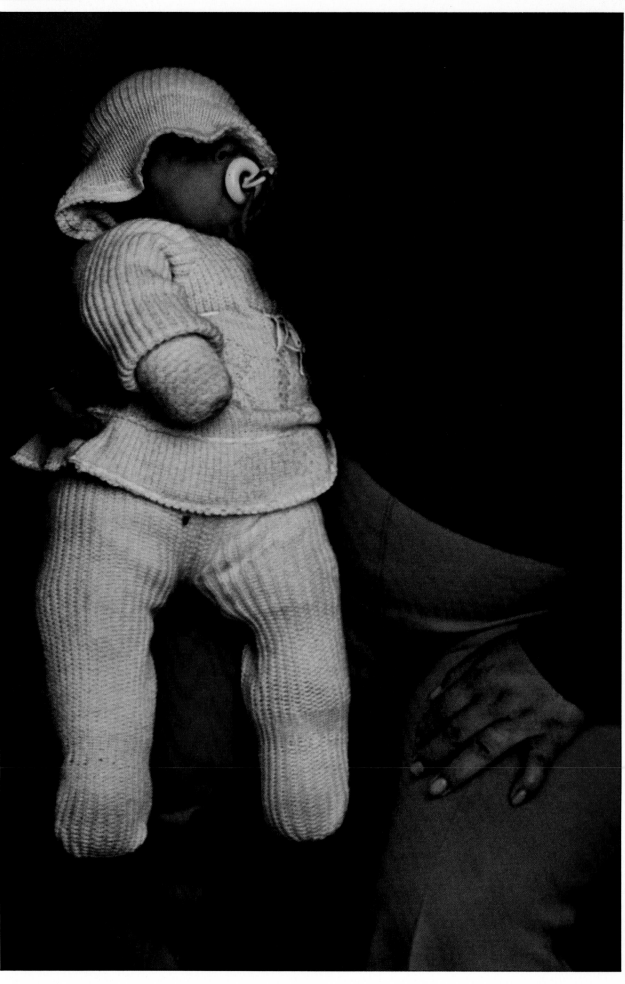

Shape and form in composition

The doll-like child was photographed in subtle lighting. I took a reading from the light-colored clothing in order to capture the delicate tonal range.

Children and animals are often considered by professional photographers to be difficult subjects. They both give of their best over very short periods and yet, whether separately or in combination, they provide challenging and appealing subjects for all photographers. The boy and his cat together form a stable triangular shape but there is an element of tension.

Shape and form are two of the most important aspects of the physical character of an object, whether it is a person, something found in nature or something man-made. They are also two important components unifying the composition of a picture. Using them effectively can transform a snapshot into an interesting and original image. In child photography, however, the advantages of careful composition must always be weighed against the need to work quickly if you are to capture a fleeting expression or a momentous event, such as your child's first steps. The spirit of the photograph is always more important than the structure.

Shape is two-dimensional: it is an outline of an object without the content or depth. At its simplest and most dramatic, it can be a profile head in full silhouette. Lighting and camera viewpoint all play their part in using shape to give interest and structure to a picture.

The strongest shape can be that provided by the subject, as in the picture (right) where the baby provides an interesting triangular shape. Contrasting the subject against a plain background or against the light emphasizes shape and makes it more powerful in the composition. Alternatively, the dominant shape can contain an image within its form that contrasts both in shape and texture. The photograph of the little girl wearing a straw hat (previous page) is held together by the embracing outline of the wicker chair.

Form is the descriptive element of an object. It gives visual clues to its character and texture, solidity being conveyed by gradations in tone from light to dark. The contrast of light and shadow areas transforms the two-dimensional into three dimensions. Every lighting condition shows us form in a different way and it should be in accord with the form—soft light for delicate tonal qualities, harsh light for drama.

The first steps are among the most important stages to capture if you are making a record of a child's development. The smooth arching body of this baby makes a dominant triangular shape contrasting with the carpet and crib.

Learning to crawl is an equally significant achievement. Here I have caught the precise moment of collapse after a triumphant few feet. A plain background sets off the sprawled shape of the child.

Though still a baby, this child was minding a stall in a market of the former Congolese capital, Elizabethville. I wanted to convey the child's vulnerability as well as the scale of his problem and so I took a closeup using a wide-angle lens so that the child appears as an anxious appendage to the bowl.

The strained pose of the South African boy, who had asked to have his photograph taken, reflects and emphasizes the uncertainty and tension in his face.

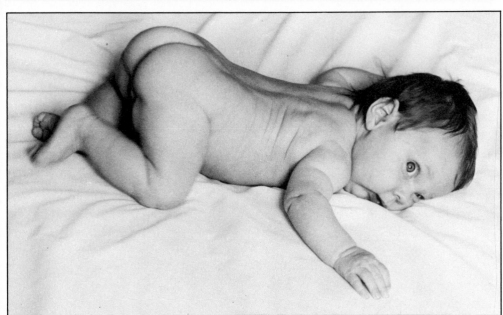

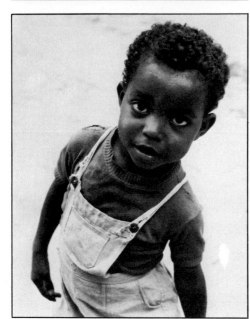

Every element recorded in a photograph contributes to its success or failure. The shape and positioning of children, their environment, and their clothes (especially the colors), and the quality of light are often as important as gestures and facial expressions. The vibrant colors frequently used in children's clothing are not always easy to handle but can be used to convey the boisterous energy and extrovert nature of some children or, by contrast, to highlight the meek demeanor of more timid children.

The Portuguese girl, photographed in her neat party dress, conveys, despite her self-consciousness, a strong feeling of repose. The blues in her dress supported by grey tones harmonize with the blue cast of the concrete floor and are a perfect foil for the delicate tones of her face.
Leicaflex, 50 mm, 1/60, f11, Ektachrome 64.

The vulnerability of the little Indonesian girl has been emphasized by the strong color of her dress isolated in a subdued background. While the use of a long lens has slightly exaggerated the contrast in proportion, overcast conditions have helped create the impression of a harsh environment.
Pentax, 200 mm, 1/500, f5.6, Ektachrome 200.

Color and tone in composition

Color and harmony in the girl's clothing and background, and the uncomplicated composition have contributed to this powerful and sympathetic portrait.

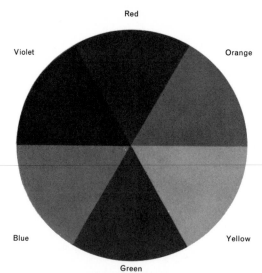

The circle indicates the way in which colors register as tone when recorded by black and white film. In color photography, you can use color harmony and contrast to compose your pictures. In black and white photography, it is graduations of tone, shown here as a continuous shading from black to white, that provide the modelling and contrast which are such important elements in composition.

Though enthusiasts argue the respective merits of color and black and white photography, each has its own qualities and strengths. You may prefer to record children in full color but it is a serious mistake to think of black and white as a poor alternative.

In black and white photography, color as well as shadow and light are reduced to a range of tones varying from black through to white. It is the variation of tone that gives objects their form. Harmonizing these tonal qualities in a picture is one of the most effective ways of achieving the illusion of volume and depth. The delicacy and lightness of high-key pictures—those in which light tones predominate—are often considered particularly suited for photographs of children. However, there are no infallible rules. Low-key pictures—ones in which dark tones predominate—can produce highly dramatic images. For most pictures the photographer will want to record a full range of tones in order to render the modelling with maximum subtlety. Exposure, development and printing are all factors that, combined with the ability to see a picture, finally create an interesting tonal balance.

In color photography, the color itself introduces a dominating compositional element to photography. Used with discrimination and understanding, color can produce effects of great emotional as well as aesthetic power. What the photographer must consider is the way colors combine. Exploiting the harmony of closely related colors and hues can produce images of gentle subtlety. A random assembly of color, on the other hand, produces confusing and jumbled images. However, using contrasting colors can be a way of adding emphasis to your subject or of giving drama to an action. Experiment using large areas of single color, spots of brilliant color, gentle monochromatic studies or the vibrant contrast of discordant color.

To capture the indulgent satisfaction of this boy eating a luscious fruit, I wanted to record the modelling about his mouth with maximum clarity. Diffused light and fine grain film have allowed me to compose a picture consisting of a subtle range of middle tones.

The pleasure of messing about in boats is powerfully evoked by this picture, which contains not only large areas of white and deep shadows but also a subtle range of middle tones. Though the light areas convey the luminosity of the water and the shadows give a feeling of depth and substance, it is the grey tones that link and balance them.

Playing areas, schools, homes and gardens, in fact most places where children behave spontaneously and energetically, usually have eye-catching backgrounds. These structural and decorative elements, often highly patterned, can be incorporated as integral parts of lively and intriguing pictures of children. When, however, patterned backgrounds are not carefully related to the activity or expression of children, the subject can be completely overwhelmed.

Interiors such as school gyms and dancing studios can be particularly difficult environments in which to photograph. However, rather than exclude the potentially distracting background of a gymnasium, I have used the rigid horizontal pattern of the wall bars as a contrast to the fragile form of the small girl. *Minolta, 50 mm, 1/60, f4, Ektachrome 200.*

The expression and positioning of the little girl have linked her to the powerfully striped background in a way that no amount of manipulation could have achieved. Because my camera was pre-set, I was able to capture the instant when the strongly patterned background and subject were fully integrated without having to hesitate to make adjustments. *Pentax, 50 mm, 1/250, f8, Ektachrome 200.*

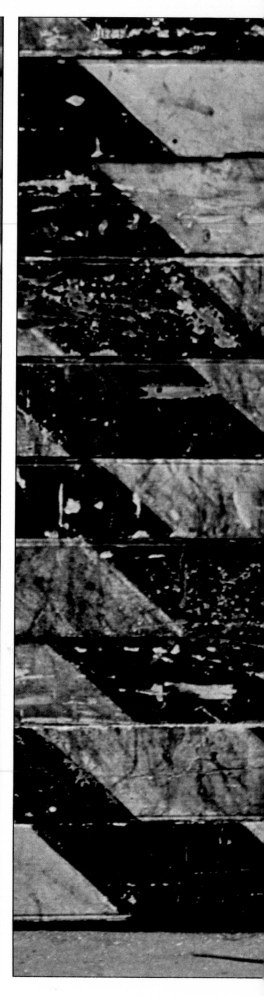

Background pattern in composition

Background pattern can add interest and vitality to your pictures of children provided it does not overwhelm the main subject.

Sharp or blurred, strong or receding, backgrounds are important because of the way they relate to the subject. The experienced photographer uses them, the amateur often finds they overwhelm his subjects. They are always there but often the eye is able to select or ignore them when taking the picture whereas the camera simply records them in all their detail and distraction. The photographer must train the eye to see potential problems in backgrounds because they are an integral part of the picture, they set the scene and they are vital when planning its construction.

As a general rule there should be one subject only and all other elements in the picture should be subordinate but supporting. If the background overpowers the intended subject the results will be muddled and disappointing.

Occasionally this rule can be broken, for example when your subject is arranged to merge into the background, its discovery giving the photograph an element of surprise. The picture of the burned-out barn (above left, opposite page) is a clear illustration of how, in this case, foreground can be used as a camouflage.

Strong plain backgrounds can be used in stark contrast to emphasize a subject or mood. They isolate the subject's shape or heighten the detail. The little boy with the cardboard mask (right) is much more dramatic because he is against a plain background, and the two boys against the white building (far right) become silhouette shapes.

Backgrounds with a strong repetitive pattern are more difficult to control because they can often be too powerful and dominate the subject. Used carefully, though, a pattern can establish a motif, or bring order and rhythm to an otherwise static photograph. Patterns in black and white tend to add an abstract quality but in color they create an emotional response of order and harmony.

Disordered pattern, that is pattern with a strong random element in it, can also have strength and unity, or it can be counterproductive and overwhelm the subject. Achieving a balance between the disordered background and the subject is usually a matter of proportion, and personal choice plays a vital part.

The waif-like fragility of this small girl is enhanced by the rough textured wall behind her. The linear pattern of the bricks also serves to emphasize her delicately patterned clothes.

The arrogant pose of this young boy is the strength of this picture. His face is hidden and the light background gives no further information but its bleakness complements the stance.

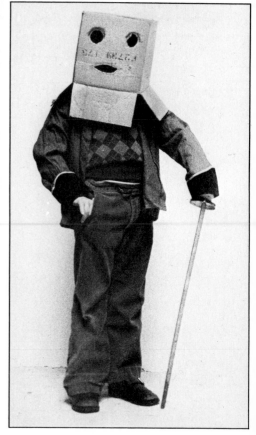

An **elaborately patterned** background competes with the girl's shower cap but they are both forced into a subordinate rôle by the powerful and surprising nature of the girl's face. The picture works because the eye is drawn immediately to her face and is not diverted to the pattern.

A flat lighting effect on the burned-out barn in snow has created an intriguing random pattern. It momentarily hides the girl on a dappled horse within the structure but, after a closer look, the strong verticals and horizontals form a clear framework for the subject.

A small boy potter in Sri Lanka sits surrounded by his work. Both the beautiful shapes of the bowls in the foreground and the dark silhouette of the ox in the back are essential in revealing the boy's lifestyle. In this picture the pots are as important as the boy himself.

The cluttered façade of a service station provides an excellent example of how random pattern occurs in everyday life. Against this background the two children and three dogs almost disappear because both subjects and background have the same degree of emphasis.

The strong shape of the building stands out clearly within the picture area causing the two boys to become silhouettes and blotting out the landscape. The contrasting black and white convey the feeling of a hot bright day.

Photographers frequently fail to achieve a balance of subject and setting, children being reduced to insignificant dots in vast landscapes or, alternatively, the background being totally excluded. By choosing the appropriate lens— either to increase the field of view or to minimize it by enlarging the subject image—and by selecting the best camera angle, it is usually fairly simple to take pictures in which the subject and the background are fully integrated.

Children derive fun and excitement from repeating their activities, which gives the photographer time and opportunity to choose the best way to relate the subject to the background. Composition, lighting and color have combined to relate these two energetic boys to the steep hillside they climbed again and again for the pleasure of running down.
Pentax, 90 mm, 1/250, f8, Kodachrome 64.

The flute player in the impressive Inca ruins at Cuzco, Peru, was photographed in the evening, when most tourists had gone and the light was fading to a warm glow. I positioned myself so as to isolate the boy's gentle but vertical shape against the hard outline of the most massive stones, thus achieving maximum contrast.
Pentax, 50 mm, 1/60, f16, Ektachrome 200.

Using strong backgrounds

Background and figures harmoniously related capture the spirit of a scene. Making the most of backgrounds can improve the composition of pictures as well as adding interesting information to your photographs of children.

Awareness of the physical setting is the first step in producing photographs that successfully relate subject to background. The beginner is so often intent on what he wants to see in the viewfinder that the background elements that can make or mar a photograph are completely neglected. In this way, faults are unconsciously included: there may be poles that seem to sprout from heads, splashes of color that dominate the picture or a clutter of detail that distracts from the subject. It is even more likely that the novice will fail to see the positive features of a background that can be used to enhance the technique of photographing children.

In photojournalism and documentary photography, background is often used with powerful effect to give an insight into widely varying social and economic conditions. In family photographs, its purpose is not likely to be so serious and yet the information a background supplies enlarges the value of these photographs as records of children in a particular place at a particular time. A background can say a lot about the personalities and interests of children. It may be a way of making

The loneliness of this little Hebridean girl, photographed on the island of North Uist, is powerfully conveyed by the harsh landscape in the background. By using a shallow depth of field, I have kept the children in focus but lessened the impact of the background, which otherwise would have been too complicated and dominant. The subject is thrust forward but is, nonetheless, part of her environment.

The amusing pairing of boy and statue, photographed in a formal Italian garden, represents the kind of unposed photograph that is a happy reminder of holidays. A posed photograph, with the child simply standing beside the statue, might have been dull. The link between the child's eyes and the mysterious heavenward gaze of the statue has drawn the two together in the picture and introduced an element of fun.

clear what activity children are engaged in or it may explain a particular grouping of people. It can also convey the special atmosphere of memorable occasions.

With holiday photographs, the prime motive will often be to record children in relation to the landscapes and monuments they are visiting as tourists. The photograph is a way of saying "I have been there", but you should always aim for more than just a blunt record. In taking travel photographs, it is frequently better to think of how the inclusion of a child or group of children can en-hance a picture of another subject. They may simply provide a useful indication of scale, but they can be used to bring life to an otherwise static picture.

Whatever the importance of the information conveyed by the background, it must be used with discrimination to enhance the aesthetic value of a picture. In any situation there is almost certainly a variety of options that will produce interesting pictures. The most obvious does not necessarily produce the best photograph so it is always worth trying more than one approach.

The choice of lens allows a considerable degree of flexibility. Even with a standard lens, the photographer has plenty of scope for altering the relationship of subject to background by manipulating the aperture and so changing the depth of field. A shallow depth of field can soften what would otherwise be a dominating background and yet allow it to convey all the information that is needed. The photographer's greatest asset, however, will always be an alert eye and a willingness to look at potential material from as many angles as possible.

Monkey and girl, photographed in Indonesia, form another amusing contrast, the old-man look of the monkey a foil for the vivacity and humor of the girl. Tourists, children just as much as adults, want straightforward evidence of their trips to faraway places. The discreet inclusion of appropriate background information, suggesting locality, season and weather, provide keys to a bank of happy memories.

The plain dress and casual posture of the girl contrast nicely with the elaborate decoration of a Moroccan mosque. This is an example of a long tradition in photography, bringing an element of life into what would otherwise be a picture of undiluted architectural detail. Though the background rather than the child is the subject, she is an integrated element giving interest and a sense of scale.

The uniformed girls in a convent school asked to be photographed and within a few minutes had formed themselves into a visually satisfying group. The apparently random way in which children arrange themselves coherently can be utilized in formal and informal situations. *Pentax, 28 mm, 1/125, f8, Ektachrome 64.*

A local band performing at a fête adopted this unconventional grouping when a storm forced them to shelter under a tree. Exposing for the shadow area under the tree has given a deceptively summery impression despite the overcast conditions. *Pentax, 35 mm, 1/125, f5.6, Ektachrome 200.*

The cluster of boys imprisoned in the bright blue window frame were easy victims when I suddenly turned my camera on them as they were watching me working. *Pentax, 50 mm, 1/125, f8, Ektachrome 64.*

Hands and feet as well as faces can express a great deal about individuals and groups. With this band of Portuguese children I was attracted by the variety of their footwear and their grubby bare feet. When they asked for their photograph to be taken, I focused on their faces and then unexpectedly turned the camera on their feet before they had a chance to move. *Pentax, 28 mm, 1/250, f8, Ektachrome 200.*

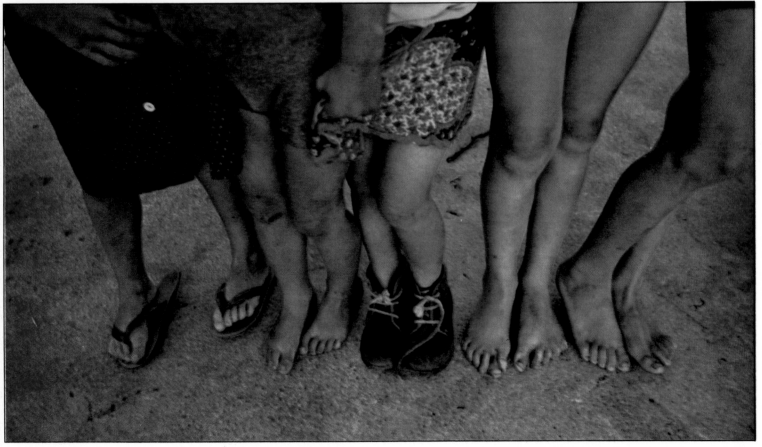

Photographing groups

A well-balanced arrangement of a large group is not always the result of the photographer positioning children individually.

The easy relationship spanning generations has been caught in this moment of intense concentration in a private game. Even though I have not included the faces of the children, the image powerfully conveys the mood of the moment.

When photographing children in groups, it is important to convey what the function of the group is, as well as arranging them in a composition that expresses the purpose of the picture. It may be an interest in common, membership of a club or similar organization, or participation in a special occasion such as a wedding. In candid photography, the link may be a very short-lived one, a momentary and unstructured involvement in a shared activity.

In formal photographs of groups, clues to the link can be provided by uniforms and sporting trophies or musical instruments. Such emblems not only help to explain the nature of the group but also provide focal points. Arranging a group to best effect requires planning—although, as the key picture (above) shows, children will sometimes group themselves satisfactorily on their own account. You need a simple, uncluttered background and a way of organizing people so that the overall scheme is attractive and nobody is obscured. With a large group, children may need to be ranked according to height, perhaps in conjunction with seating. A wide-angle lens can be useful in photographing a large group but beware of distortion at the edges of the frame.

Bounced or reflected flash will give even lighting indoors. Diffused natural lighting outdoors will mean that children do not have to strain and squint while posing nor will they be hidden in dark shadows. Even in ideal conditions, you should always take enough photographs to allow for the many occasions when at least one of a group will blink or turn a head.

In candid photographs of groups, there is not the same need to portray each individual with equal emphasis. Instead, you want to choose a moment from a continuous event so that it sums up what is happening and makes clear the link between the children involved. The climax of an activity, the instant an action is completed, may be the most exciting and significant moment, but there are no rules. The anticipation of an event or the relaxed mood after accomplishment can be as revealing as a moment of tension or concentration.

Resist the temptation to treat all your subjects frontally or in profile. As the photograph of Henry Moore and two children (top left) shows, the feeling of a moment can be expressed just as powerfully by gesture and posture as by facial expression. As with all candid photography, you must be prepared to take advantage of opportunities when they come and your approach must be imaginative and flexible. Have your camera loaded with fast film and preset for speed and exposure.

The end of the line at a holiday camp beauty contest shows a mixture of pride, bewilderment and anxious anticipation at the moment of decision. Despite their varying reaction and the linear arrangement, there is no mistaking the shared involvement of the children.

Children pestering to be photographed are often taken aback when the camera is suddenly turned on them. When I reacted to the demands of these three boys, they measured their distance in a way that reflected their degree of confidence and their position within the group.

Father and sons, forming a tight-knit group on a motorcycle, were photographed from a moving car using a relatively slow shutter speed. What attracted me to the group was the contrast between the apparent danger and the confidence of the group, particularly the little boy steering.

Smiles of victory are just breaking out as this team of girls defeats a boys' team in a friendly and untutored tug-of-war. I have used a wide-angle lens so that I could get in close to catch the varying expressions and still take in the whole team.

Photodiary/THE MIDDLE YEARS

The delicacy of a young boy's features is revealed in a reverse silhouette. An open doorway to a dark interior creates the black background, while daylight lights the boy's face naturally.
Minolta, 135 mm, 1/125, f8, Kodachrome 64.

Under her floppy hat the girl's smiling face is brightened by the reflection from the table. Her silhouette is contrasted against the garden background which I overexposed by two stops to reduce distracting detail.
Pentax, 50 mm, 1/250, f5.6, Ektachrome 64.

Low evening light created this Caribbean girl's spectacular shadow as she played. Speed was essential because a moment later the unique shape disappeared.
Pentax, 100 mm, 1/500, f8, Ektachrome 64.

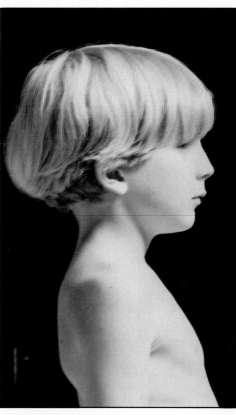

The shape of the red tricycle was the intende subject of this picture b by chance the young gir stopped to watch in sho Her shadow and her matching colors helped unify the photograph and brought it to life. The result is a more satisfyin image than of the tricycl alone.
Pentax, 28 mm, 1/250, f8, Ektachrome 64.

Strong Portuguese sun makes the group's sharply defined shadow the most powerful aspec of this picture. From directly overhead, the figures themselves are almost invisible.
Pentax, 100 mm, 1/500, f16, Ektachrome 64.

Analyzing the photographer's craft
Silhouettes and shadows

A simple but strong image is created by the contrast between the dark background and the fine, light features of a young boy.

A young rider returns home at sunset. A low camera angle close in to the horse exaggerates the shapes and distorts the head. The result is a dramatic profile against a placid sky.

Silhouettes and shadows create sharply defined shapes and areas of darkness which help make dramatic pictures. They have a sparseness and an economy of detail that is at once attractive and strong. The simplest example of a silhouette can be seen at sunset when the sun sinks behind the trees on the horizon, their outlines becoming black against the light sky. Shadows produced by figures also create focal points as forceful as (and occasionally stronger than) the subject itself.

Used in portraits of children, the silhouette can sum up a character and expression as meaningfully as an ordinary photograph by the revealing profile of the head, or even simply of the nose, chin or mouth.

The easiest way to shoot a silhouette is to place the child against a bright natural light, such as a window or door. Expose for the background only in order to lose the detail on the child. If you are printing it yourself, increase the contrast by using a hard-grade paper. Indoors, or in a studio, set the unlit subject against a white background evenly lit with two or more spotlights. Outdoors, place the subject against a bright sky and take the photograph from a low camera angle. In both situations, expose for the light background.

A reverse silhouette (see page 96), where the subject's face is fully lit and the background is dark, is an alternative which will give you a strong profile while still revealing the features.

A semi-silhouette is a compromise between the opacity of the full silhouette and the detail of the reverse silhouette. The subject is set against a light background but a side-light or reflector gives some detail and form without destroying the pure shape.

Shadow silhouettes can provide a surprising element in impromptu photographs. The picture appears more three-dimensional because the flat shadow contrasts sharply with the continuous tonal element in the pictures. Shadows, such as those of the group (on the previous page) seen from above, offer a surreal aspect, seeming almost to have a life of their own. Whether they form the subject or support it, they should not be ignored, because they provide vital descriptive elements.

Shadows must be captured without hesitation because they are constantly changing according to the angle of the sun and the quality of the surface on which the shadows fall.

Silhouettes and shadows are a rich source of ideas with which to enliven standard portraits and candid photographs. By contrast, fine detail can be accentuated and greater prominence given to areas of the picture that in direct light would have lacked significance.

The mother and child with donkey in the Sinai Desert make a picture that has a great simplicity of line and a peaceful atmosphere. It was taken at a very low camera angle against the bright sky which emphasizes the silhouettes. The stark background accentuates the figures' isolation.

Simple silhouettes can be achieved by placing the child in front of a bright window in a darkened room and a frame of tracing paper between him and the camera. This diffuses any highlight detail from the background.

The jean-clad legs of the model's sister have provided a powerful and unusual frame for the girl dressed in a brilliant harlequin costume. This mobile frame, appropriately a single color, allowed me to block out distracting peripheral highlights. At the same time, it has reinforced the shape of the subject and given the picture a sense of depth.
Pentax, 100 mm, 1/125, f5.6, Ektachrome 64.

Two children peering from the dark window of a creeper-covered building made me think of fledglings in a nest. To reinforce this idea, I deliberately included a large area of the façade and its wonderfully rich pattern of leaves. At the same time, I have taken care to omit other distracting features, such as drain-pipes and doors.
Pentax, 28 mm, 1/250, f8, Kodachrome 64.

Analyzing the photographer's craft
Framing the image

An unorthodox frame such as the one formed by legs spread apart echoes the triangular shape of the seated girl.

One of the most straightforward ways of giving interest and emphasis to your pictures is to frame the subject with subsidiary elements of the composition. Architectural features—such as archways, doorways and windows—are the most obvious, but still effective, shapes that can be used in this way. By including familiar architectural forms in photographs, their proportions can be seen in relation to, say, a child, and thus add information to the picture. As a foreground frame, they can be used to channel the view through to the subject beyond. Used in the background, their

outlines can contain and focus attention on the subject.

Architectural features are far from being the only framing devices the photographer can use, and merely giving emphasis to the main subject is not the only function a frame can perform. In simplifying pictures, the first step is to minimize clutter and distracting detail in order to give a clear view and understanding of the subject. Any object can form a frame to mask extraneous detail but a linking element that supports the subject should be sought. The range of possible objects for

The door, flanked symmetrically by windows, trees and posts (below), frames the girl and her nursemaid within another frame formed by the foreground window.

The two boys are looking out of the picture (bottom) so intently that it needs the presence of their mother, framed in the window, to arrest our gaze and hold it on them.

The contrast of sky and building reflected in the window (right) is an integral and menacing part of the frame surrounding the grandmother and child.

this purpose is almost unlimited: foliage, rocks, walls, buildings, statues or animals. A photographer can easily make his own frame by cutting holes in either plain or colored paper. I have even used a torn film carton, held a few centimeters in front of the lens, in order to mask distracting detail.

As well as obscuring unwanted detail, framing devices can also fill in uninteresting foregrounds or empty skies with color, tone and texture that contrast with or complement the subject. Overhanging branches can, for instance, close in the subject and create an evocative atmosphere. Devices of this kind are useful for masking the sun when photographing into the light. They can dramatically increase the sense of depth by suggesting a succession of receding planes.

When using a frame, and often it will be in more than one way, combine its use with selective focusing. Although the subject should be in sharp focus, generally the frame will serve its purpose best if it suggests the haziness of peripheral vision. A shallow depth of field allows the subject to be sharp and prevents the frame from overwhelming the picture. For correct exposure, take a reading for the main subject rather than a general one for the whole area. A foreground frame can be most effective by using the high contrast of a dark foreground, for example, looking through a dark archway to a gently lit subject.

Using a frame that supports the idea of the picture calls for imagination and a willingness to experiment with both the angle of view and different focal length lenses. Look at the photographs throughout this book to see what an important compositional device framing can be.

Keeping babies happy (below) may limit the angle of approach. I have made a virtue of necessity by using the crib against a dark setting as a frame.

A chair with a solid back (bottom) provides a very useful frame for photographs of young children. It cuts unwanted detail at the same time as giving the child support.

The bonnet, combining with the collar to form a decorative frame (right), sets off the face of a small child momentarily fascinated by the photographer.

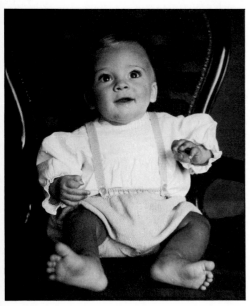

When composing a picture, one normally tries to contain the action or the spirit of the picture totally within the frame. However, there are many occasions when interesting pictures can be obtained by ignoring normal conventions. Their dynamism relies on what is implied rather than what is stated, or simply on the element of surprise.

The little girl caught at the window is an example of a simple incident which, nonetheless, has made an interesting picture. There is a rich color harmony but also an element of tension as the child struggles, feet perilously far from the ground, to peer through heavy net curtains for a glimpse of the television set, which is in the room out of sight.
Leicaflex, 50 mm, 1/125, f5.6, Kodachrome 64.

The girl and dog, one running, the other alert, are both reacting to something outside the frame, something to which the photographer might have been expected to turn his camera. The exclusion of this element rather than diminishing the force of the picture has created its mysterious tension. Other elements in the composition have also helped to heighten this tension. These include the strong diagonals, which are anchored in the firmly delineated dog and lead to the blurred movement of the girl, the spectral shadows, and the balance and linkage of tone and color.
Pentax, 28 mm, 1/30, f16, Ektachrome 64.

Experimenting with composition

The strong area of the window is an effective compositional balance to the child firmly positioned in the lower third of the frame. Our eyes follow those of the child as she gazes through the window into the room beyond. Our interest lies in the conjecture of what holds her interest.

Composition is the selection and organization of the elements of a picture into a cohesive whole that expresses the individual vision of the photographer. It enables him to relate visually his reactions to his subject, so that the viewer immediately sees the full significance of the picture. Line, shape, tone, color, texture, pattern, perspective, scale and depth are all important elements of composition. Though there are formal rules borrowed from painting, for most photographers composition is largely a matter of intuition, combined with a sense of balance and harmony.

Try to keep things simple: in general, choose a single, dominant subject in each picture and make the rest of the picture relate to and support this theme. The eye should go immediately to the main subject, then roam easily over the whole picture area—but always being led gently back to the central image. Too much going on in a picture usually results in the eye being bombarded with visual information, and the viewer becomes first confused and then bored. A well-composed picture makes a strong initial impact and then offers the opportunity to study the supportive effects.

Balance—the visual harmony between elements of shape, line, tone and color—is important. This need not imply a symmetrical arrangement: on the contrary, a useful guide (the so-called "Rule of Thirds") is to divide the picture horizontally and vertically into equal thirds and to position the key elements of the picture on or at the intersection of these divisions. This can be used to balance out the relationship between foreground, middle distance and background.

Depth relates the subject to its setting. It defines the spatial relationship between foreground and background using perspective. This is seen mainly through *linear perspective* (convergence of lines receding into the distance), *aerial perspective* (color and tone fading into the distant atmospheric haze), *diminishing scale* (objects looking smaller when further away) and *overlapping forms* (one object partially obscuring another behind it). Scale indicates the comparative size and importance of objects. Areas of mass need to be balanced against one another, since they give the overall weight or bias of a picture. Where the photographer stands in relation to his subject and the lighting on it will also have a strong effect on composition. If time permits, walk around your subject, viewing it through the viewfinder from all possible angles, to find the best viewpoint. Do not be afraid to take many shots of the same subject from different positions. Sometimes great patience is needed to wait for just the right expression or approach.

Composition in thirds has positioned the boy learning to swim firmly in the lower part of the picture. It is at once obvious what the main subject is, but the rest of the shot is still of strong relevance: the earnest expression of the boy links closely with the watchful eye of his teacher, and the receding continuous tone leads us gradually from the foreground towards the background figure.

The child's face, and thus the focus of our attention, is to one side of the frame. But see how the direction of the boy's glance, and the curve of his thumb, automatically lead us to the left. The vertical lines make our eyes rove over the rough boards, contrasting their texture with the smoothness of the boy's skin, until we are compulsively drawn back to the eyes once again.

Linear perspective, the diminishing lines and planes converging in the distance, highlights the positioning of this girl in a long corridor. This tunnel effect and the highly symmetrical arrangement concentrate our attention on her exclusively.

Aerial perspective relates foreground to middle distance and background. Other riders give an illusion of depth through diminishing size. The bathers are sandwiched between foreground and dominant industrial background.

Low camera angle gives strength to this shot of a boy with his toy dump truck, emphasizing its power and strength. Shooting up into the shadow area makes the toy look more substantial. The line of trees helps this vertical thrust. In this kind of picture we are entering the child's imagination and treating toys as if they were full size. If we tilt the camera, we give an illusion of speed to a stationary go-cart. Depth and the distance covered are suggested by the track's curve.

Highlights and deep shadows contrast strongly in this picture, dividing the image horizontally into roughly equal areas of foreground, middle distance and background, giving an atmosphere of repose in an idyllic setting. The boy and his bicycle are positioned off center, their shapes highlighted against an abstract background. The foreground shadow leads the eye via the tree trunk into the dark foliage of the background, framing the cyclist.

Holiday pictures should capture the relaxed mood and spontaneity of children, their sense of freedom and the excitement of new places. Have your camera with you at all times so that you do not miss vital moments: when it is always there, children ignore it and behave quite naturally. The perfect photograph, in terms of technique and composition, may be difficult to take on a crowded beach bathed in brilliant sunshine but what will make your photographs worthwhile is the way they capture the liveliness of your own children and of other children about you. Be careful not to underexpose faces. Reflected light from sand and sea can give deceptively high exposure readings. Remember that seawater and sand are potentially harmful to your camera. Take every reasonable precaution to protect your equipment and make sure it is adequately insured in case of loss or theft.

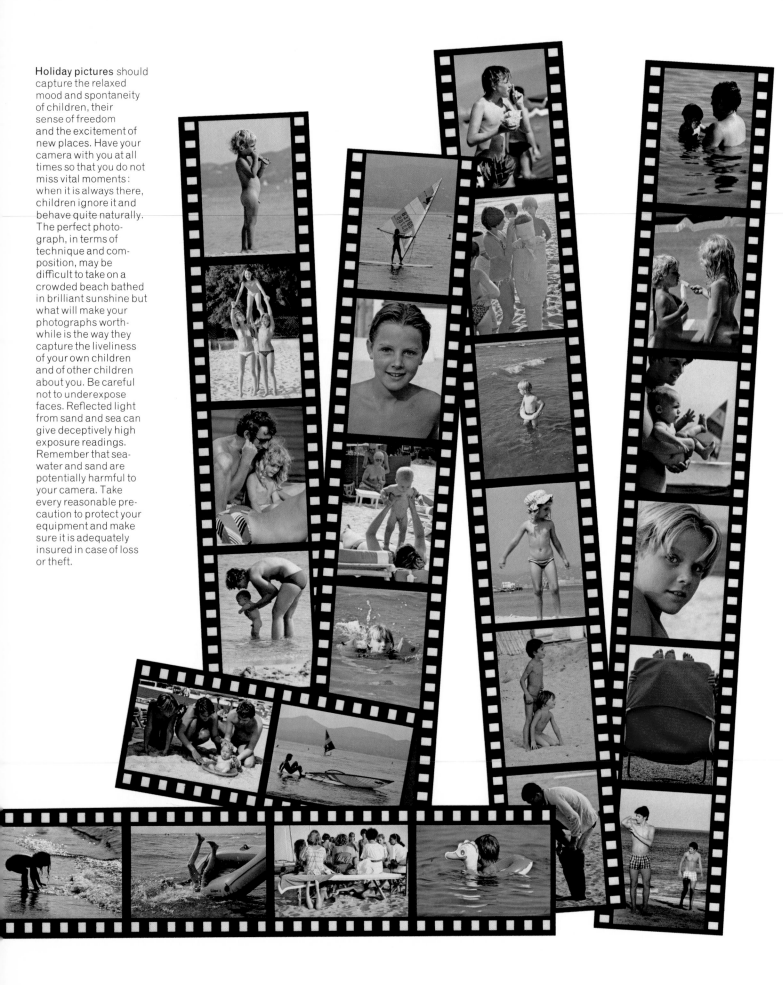

Cropping for impact

A candid shot taken on a beach becomes a more intimate portrait when cropped to remove an unwanted person in the background. It reveals the sinuous quality of the girl's body which contrasts with her childish pose.

A photograph can be composed for better effect in many ways. Here, a portrait of a mother and young baby is shown cropped in landscape and portrait formats. Both are successful because the distracting background and lower half of the mother have been removed and the eye goes straight to the facial expressions of the two subjects.

When taking a photograph, the photographer has many considerations before pressing the shutter. One of the most important of these is composition: also shape, form, texture, color and tone, as well as the overall harmony, contrast, balance and rhythm. The experienced photographer tries to develop an "eye" for the requirements that will enable him to compose and take shots instantly because, in general, it is best to compose pictures within the frame formed by the viewfinder. Some photographers find that using the hands to frame the shot before taking it (see illustration above) helps rule out unnecessary clutter. Occasionally, however, there just is not time to consider every aspect, or to change the lens or position and, in these situations, the photographer can resort to cropping the picture afterwards in the darkroom.

Cropping in this sense means selecting only part of a negative to enlarge for the final picture. In order to give yourself more freedom to do this, when taking the photograph allow a good area of background around the subject.

Whether a picture is cropped closer before it is taken or afterwards, cropping helps simplify a picture by cutting out distracting detail; it allows greater importance to be given to the subject and causes the eye to be directed to the focal point. Always think before taking any picture—have I included any unnecessary elements?

Since life does not always arrange itself to fit the camera's format (even when there is time to compose the shot), cropping gives you a second chance to perfect or change the emphasis of a picture. It helps to improve the candid shot taken because the mood, light or subject was suddenly right, even though the entire composition was imperfect. Perhaps it was marred by an unwanted item in the background or distracting highlights.

If your picture does need cropping after you have taken it, place L-shaped frames (illustrated above) to block off the unwanted areas on the contact print (or the full-sized print). Draw in the area required on the print and use it as a guide for the enlargement. Enlarge the new image to the desired size and shape.

When applied successfully, cropping is a useful tool of the photographer but it is no substitute for careful preparation and insight.

Horseback riding is a passion with many teenage girls. Here, the speed of the horse's gallop is captured by a fast exposure and emphasized by the way the picture has been cropped. The long narrow shape suggests energetic forward motion and high velocity.

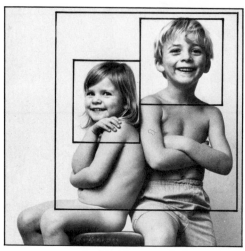
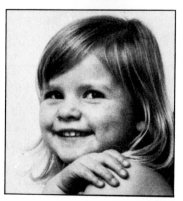

A good group portrait with all subjects responding is a rare thing where children are concerned. This is where cropping is particularly useful and, as seen right, smaller pictures can intensify the focus of attention on the child as an individual. Alternatively, if you find that your picture is fundamentally sound but that it has distracting areas of clothing, color or limb positions, these can also be cropped out to good effect.

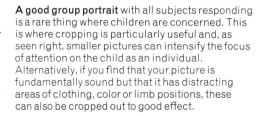

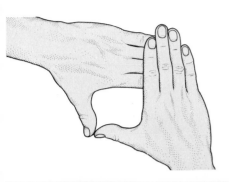

Most photographers compose the potential shot through the viewfinder. Alternatively, they hold their hands (far left) in front of their eyes as a viewfinder. This helps remove superfluous detail and reveals any imbalances. After you have taken the photograph, you can further crop it by using two right-angled black L-shapes (left) to mask off the unwanted areas on the contact print before enlarging the negative.

A beautiful child in Sri Lanka was photographed with a normal lens from a distance (left), in order not to disturb her wistful expression. By going in closer or changing lenses I would probably have disturbed the child and missed this shot, so a solution was to take it and then to crop out the unnecessary background afterwards. The result (above) is, in fact, a much more dramatic and sensitive image.

A distant group of small girls (above) seems lost in the long empty alleyway and their characters are impossible to detect. By making a closer crop (below) the attractive lines of cobblestones still take the eye into the picture but now the girls' smiling faces bring life into it. We can also see that the middle girl is being taught to rollerskate. The picture could also have been cropped to make a vertical, or portrait shape, which would have emphasized the narrow alleyway.

Dramatic moods and emotions of children, which show so clearly and immediately in their faces, change from laughter to tears and back again with astonishing rapidity. In photographing children, capturing a significant moment is what matters, even when it means that a picture is not quite perfect technically or compositionally. To record the shifting play of personality and feelings in the features of children, the photographer has to shoot in an instant. With a shutter speed of 1/125 or more you will be able to catch fleeting expressions provided you are alert enough to seize the opportunity when it comes. For head shots, I prefer to use a lens in the 90—135 mm range as it means you can fill the frame without crowding the subject and without getting a distorted image. Using a standard lens can mean that you are standing disconcertingly close to the subject and possibly putting your own shadow onto your model. However, there are no inflexible rules—the boy at the bottom right of the selection (left) was taken at close range with a 28 mm wide-angle. As this selection shows, these children are rarely self-conscious, even when looking at the camera.

Waiting for smiles and laughter should not cause you to miss the display of other emotions, such as an all-consuming if fleeting moment of unhappiness. The little boy (right) is totally absorbed in expressing his despair, yet a moment later he was laughing happily. The portrait was taken inside using light from a window.
Pentax, 100 mm, 1/125, f5.6, Ektachrome 64.

Capturing the moment

The most powerful photographs of children record the play of expression and emotion on their faces. Be prepared to shoot at once when the right moment comes—it may not be repeated.

Children are made for candid photography, displaying a fascinating range of emotions that makes superb subject matter. A single session—or even sequence—can produce a full range of human emotion, from pathos to rage. Although children frequently play to the camera, the novelty can soon fade and they will return to normal behavior. If they do not, stand further back and change to a long-focus lens. Alternatively, take a series and leave a few exposures in reserve. Announce that you have finished and resume shooting the moment they relax.

Children are natural performers and may defy your efforts to obtain spontaneous reactions. Turn this to advantage—their posturing can produce interesting results. Even the opposite reaction of shyness, sometimes encountered when the photographer is a stranger, can produce captivating photographs. As a last resort bribery, flattery, cajolery or cunning may be necessary.

Setting up an ideal situation in which children are encouraged to participate in a specified activity is a rewarding way of getting lively and interesting pictures. After supplying the impetus, give them

A noisy game of cards was in progress while I was reading in the garden. The commotion made concentration impossible. It was easier to photograph it than fight it, so I took this sequence recording the children's total involvement in the activity, and the changing pattern of triumph and disappointment. Such sequences should be picture stories. It is unnecessary for each shot to feature a dramatic moment—the calmer moments have their place in a faithful record of the activity as a whole.

"Boy with cello" could be a formal portrait—but I was interested by the subject's almost dream-like absorption in the music. Natural light from the side picks out the strong shape of the instrument and highlights the face and hands.

Children love painting and there is endless potential in turning them loose with paints and blank paper. The contrast of attitudes is striking—the girl on the left is stretching to the limit, the boy has lost interest and the other girl expresses lively curiosity at what is happening around her.

total freedom and wait until they become absorbed before starting to shoot. Never force children to cooperate—their natural instincts are usually sufficient. I prefer photographs of children to be activity-based, illustrating their relationship to the activity and reason for being involved. I continue shooting until I feel the potential of the situation is exhausted.

Where children are the subject, the photographer requires quick reflexes and rarely has the chance to reset camera controls. Children move very fast, so it is important to be prepared. Diffused lighting allows maximum flexibility, and exposure may be preset. Weak sun or light overcast sky are ideal for outdoor work, while indoor sessions work best with an overall light source. Even when children wander about, the photographer does not need to make constant exposure adjustment.

Taking account of prevailing light conditions, use a film that allows shutter speeds of at least 1/125, preferably 1/250 seconds. This enables you to catch spontaneous movement and quick reactions. It is often impossible to use fast shutter speeds inside, in which case flash is preferable to bright studio lighting, which can take some time to set up and may make children self-conscious. Remember, though, that young babies can be frightened by flash.

I often use a wide aperture setting to create a shallow depth of field, bringing the subject in to sharp focus and blurring conflicting background that would otherwise detract from the effect. I also carry a second camera, preset for the conditions, in case I run out of film at a crucial moment. There is nothing more annoying than missing such a moment—once passed, it is gone forever.

School work obviously interests the girl on the right. I emphasized her complete concentration by bringing her face into sharp focus but stopping right down to f2 to give a narrow depth of field. The selection of a specific area of interest is reinforced by the simple tonal effect of the extraneous content.

The music lesson (below left) was awkward to expose, with the main subject area between two windows. However, I like the relationship of figures, surroundings and activity, which provide an integrated picture. The child's emotions cannot be judged, but her teacher's reaction is sufficient clue.

Another music lesson —this time Sri Lankan style—has a strong triangular composition. The position of the teacher at the apex is stressed by the low angle of view. The drummer is performing confidently. The teacher watches the boy on the right, who is much less sure of his performance.

Children mimicking the behavior and gestures of adults provide the photographer with many opportunities for interesting photographs. It is essential to work quickly because manly stance and defiant gesture, for example, can change in an instant to a lighthearted response. Always include sufficient background to make clear the purpose of a child's action and to set the scene of the activity.

The self-confident, firm stance of the boy seems to depend on the sense of security the rifle has given him. Whatever the cow might do, the boy is in complete control. His position, forming a cross at the center of an exceptionally three-dimensional picture, reinforces his formidable posture. The sense of depth has been created by the road, which draws the eye in along the interrupted line, and the succession of horizontals formed by the cow

and the shadows created by strong side-lighting. The right-hand line echoes the central line of the road and seems like another barrier to the movement of the cow.
Pentax, 50 mm, 1/500, f5.6, Kodachrome 64.

The guard at the château gates is a little French boy brandishing a rifle to block our way in. He wields the rifle in a manlike way but at the same time childishly hides behind it, using it to cover his eyes. The colorful clothing completes the impression of a sentry warning us not to step from the dark shadow of the gateway into the bright light of the courtyard.
Leicaflex, 50 mm, 1/500, f5.6, Kodachrome 64.

Presetting the camera

The dynamic quality of this photograph depends on the precise positioning of boy and cow, which I was able to capture by recognizing the potential of the situation and acting quickly.

Capturing unusual moments may be partly chance, but for the good photographer it becomes instinctive to be in the right place at the right time. It is also a matter of awareness, of guessing how the situation is likely to develop, and being ready to use the camera with a minimum of adjustment in order to capture spontaneous actions that appeal. Having the camera preset and loaded with fast film will provide maximum flexibility. Automatic cameras can be a help in rapidly changing conditions, but make allowances if shooting against the light, or pictures will be underexposed.

The girl on the clothesline was part of a group of children playing in a neighbor's garden, encouraging each other to more and more exciting and dangerous activities. When children are aware of the camera, as here, they are often spurred to extravagant and comic behavior which, nonetheless, can be very revealing.

Regular weight checks for young babies take place in the butcher's shop in this remote Northumberland village. Mothers with babies to weigh take their place in the line of regular shoppers buying meat. Forewarned, I came in inconspicuously and captured a bizarre scene, giving another meaning to "family butcher".

Photodiary/THE ENERGY OF CHILDREN

The vitality of children is often best expressed by including an element of movement in the subject. Panning (swinging the camera during exposure) creates background "speed lines", which increase the sense of motion and speed.

By vertically panning the camera, I was able to convey the movement of the boy on a trampoline. The artificial lighting in the gymnasium limited available shutter speeds and apertures. *Pentax, 50 mm, 1/15, f3.5, Ektachrome 200.*

The liveliness of the Peruvian boy is effectively conveyed by the contrast of blurred and sharply defined areas. A faster shutter speed would have frozen all movement on the boy. *Pentax, 50 mm, 1/60, f16, Ektachrome 200.*

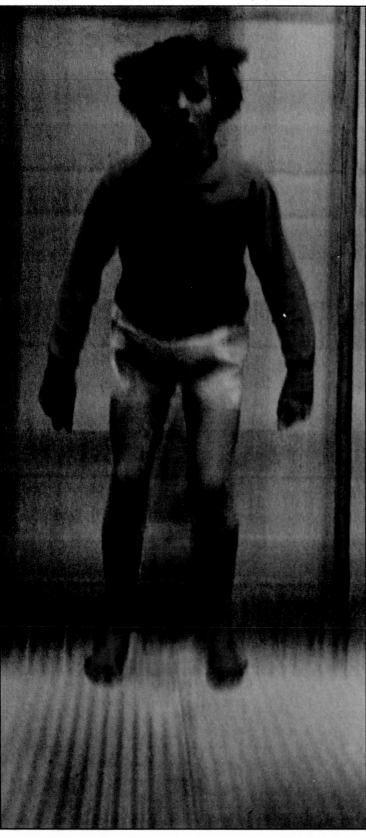

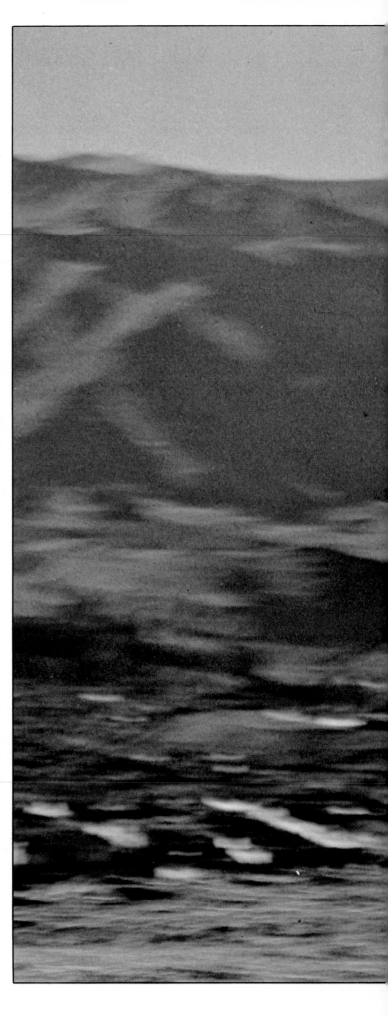

The use of panning

Panning movement should follow the subject. I used a vertical pan for the child bouncing on a trampoline.

The dancer's motion was arrested by a shutter speed of 1/1000. The low angle exaggerates the size and importance of the dancer in relation to the room, and her graceful midair position is sufficient statement of her movement.

The technique of stopping a fast-moving subject by the use of fast shutter speeds enables the photographer to record movement accurately in a way the human eye cannot. While a subject frozen in mid-action can communicate the nature of movement in various ways, the result is sometimes disappointing. Moving subjects tend to lose the sense of motion against the sharply defined details of a static background, relying totally on the position and character of the subject to express movement. This technique can work—as shown by the photograph of the dancer (left)—but there are other ways of communicating the idea of movement and vitality.

By following a moving object with the camera—panning in a horizontal arc in line with the subject's movement, releasing the shutter at the chosen moment and continuing to pan smoothly—the result will be a clear image of the subject against a blurred background. While the principle is straightforward, each shot will be governed by circumstances—the subject's speed, path, distance from the camera and desired result.

Panning offers endless scope for the creation of striking photographs. Consider the purpose of the action you are recording and decide if there is a moment that sums it up: a child at the apex of his swing, for example. In such a picture the chance element always plays a part—it could be the angle of the swing, the contrasting background or the

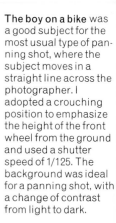

A garden swing always attracts children and makes an ideal subject for the use of panning technique. In this case it enabled me to record the expression of the boy in sharp detail. To capture the spirit of the swing's movement I panned in an arc that followed its progress. I kept the viewfinder firmly on the boy's face. The setting was 1/30 at f16. This resulted in speed lines on the pullover of the boy in the foreground which add to the sense of movement.

The boy on a bike was a good subject for the most usual type of panning shot, where the subject moves in a straight line across the photographer. I adopted a crouching position to emphasize the height of the front wheel from the ground and used a shutter speed of 1/125. The background was ideal for a panning shot, with a change of contrast from light to dark.

A firm stance is required for successful panning. Set the exposure and focus on the chosen point in advance. Frame the moving subject as soon as possible and pan with a smooth movement, turning the body from the waist up to follow the subject. Release the shutter as the subject passes and continue to pan without interrupting the smooth movement.

movement of the child's body that makes it successful. In such photographs, the chance element always plays a part. The unforeseen is an exciting aspect of photography. It is always worth experimenting with the effects of slight blur, especially if the subject is rather pedestrian. In composing, a speeding cyclist may be more effective to one side of the picture area, emphasizing the feeling of fast movement over a given distance. The relationship of subject and background must also be considered—a lone runner can be panned against a large landscape to stress the solitary nature of the activity, or shot in closeup to convey the physical effort involved. By selecting a slow shutter speed, the subject itself may be slightly blurred, becoming an identifiably defined but undetailed image that effectively communicates the excitement of the moment, such as a hurdler at full stretch or a soccer player making a tackle.

The direction of a panning shot should follow the subject. The most usual pan is where the subject is moving across the photographer's viewpoint in a straight path. Vertical panning was necessary with the child on a trampoline. Action can be reinforced by angling the shot so the subject's stability becomes unbalanced. Following the subject through the viewfinder, the subject-to-lens distance will be changing all the time. Either stop down to give increased depth of field or focus in advance on the spot where you feel it is most likely

the moving subject will be photographed. The closer you are to a moving subject the faster the shutter speed needed to reveal detail.

The blurred speed lines that emphasize movements in panning shots, giving them much of their character, are caused by the moving camera drawing highlights across shadows or vice versa. It is therefore necessary to select a background with contrast between light and dark areas to take maximum advantage of the possibilities. The slower the pan, the longer the speed lines will be. A standard lens is good for panning shots because it is easy to handle. If a longer lens is necessary to cover a sports event, consider using a tripod with panning tilt head for smoother action.

Panning is one technique where the SLR is not ideal, because the subject is invisible through the viewfinder at the crucial moment of exposure. For this reason I often use a direct-view camera when panning. It is possible to get an auxiliary frame finder for attachment to the accessory shoe of an SLR, which helps overcome the problem by allowing the subject to remain in view throughout the operation. The TLR is awkward for panning use—it has the disconcerting characteristic of reversing the subject's direction of travel in the viewfinder, and waist-level panning is difficult. However, many TLR cameras are fitted with a sports finder which folds out of the hood, permitting direct framing and eye-level use.

The shutter speed will vary with the speed and distance of the subject. As a guide, most movement can be panned at 1/15 or 1/30 to give a sharp subject image and blurred background. Fast-moving objects like cars may require 1/60 or 1/125, and it is possible to achieve a blurred background at 1/250 if the panning movement is fast enough. Use the slowest speed possible—it is desirable to use a small aperture to give greater depth of field, making it easier to frame and hold the subject.

It is quite possible to "stage" a panning shot if you have control over the subject. Children are usually willing to cooperate enthusiastically on such a project. The action may be repeated over and over again, allowing you to plan the shot and try alternative angles of view and shutter speeds. It is possible to experiment in the same way with certain subjects that cannot be controlled—for example, a race where contestants lap the track several times. An advanced use of panning is the communication of a sense of movement through the creation of pattern alone. This is particularly effective in color photography where colors and hues can be merged together to produce beautiful color effects.

Mastery of panning takes time and practice, but the effort is worth while. Once the basic technique is properly understood, panning may be used to create many exciting pictures.

Photodiary/MAGIC MOMENTS

Electronic flash has effectively caught the movement of the girl striding towards me. By using a slow shutter speed and swinging the camera through an arc during exposure, I produced an interesting background, radial lines carrying highlights into shadow. *Pentax, 50 mm, 1/15, f22, Ektachrome 200.*

The surrealistic image of the boy was achieved using electronic flash on an automatic camera operating at a fast shutter speed and metering for the foreground. The dart hangs immobilized against a darkened sky, the writing on the dart clearly visible. *Vivitar, 24 mm, automatic, Ektachrome 64.*

Flash for speed

Speed lines in the background add to the sense of movement, while electronic flash has effectively frozen the girl in mid-stride.

A dramatic silhouette (below) was the result when I used 1/500 at f8 on a dull day—the speed required to freeze all movement.

The correct exposure to capture detail in these conditions was 1/125 at f2. This would not have stopped the action, so I used daylight flash at f11 and exposed for the highlight of the boy's face. The speed of the flash froze the dart, and revealed details of features clearly.

In the failing light, it would have been impossible to freeze the skateboarder's rapid motion without flash. I selected my spot, set the camera and awaited the right moment. In the photograph below, I underexposed the sky, making an effective dark background for the figure.

The possibilities of recording movement can be extended by the use of daylight flash. In light conditions that do not permit the setting of a shutter speed fast enough to freeze movement, electronic flash (which at short distances may produce a flash with a duration of 1/300 to 1/10,000 of a second or less) can be used. The duration of the flash rather than shutter speed determines exposure and the movement arrested.

When photographing children in action, flash can serve a dual purpose. It stops movement and, when shooting against the light, helps fill in detail of the subject that might otherwise be lost and result in a silhouette effect. The use of flash on moving subjects in daylight, in conjunction with slow shutter speeds, produces a combination of detail and blurring that adds to the sense of movement. This is caused by the recording of small amounts of ambient light.

Synchronized electronic flash may also be used to create unusual results when photographing certain types of moving subject—high-speed machinery, water from a hose, a bag of flour hitting the ground, a girl at full gallop on a horse—with a clarity that cannot be achieved by the human eye, which records the composite movement rather than its individual elements.

It is possible to achieve good results in these areas with a simple camera, providing it is possible to synchronize for electronic flash. Flash bulbs, with arc duration of about 1/50 second, are less effective, taking longer to reach maximum brightness and dying away less quickly.

The combination of flash and daylight works well in color—electronic flash has the same color temperature as daylight, and discrepancies are minimal. For portrait work—against a bright sky, for example, where flash is required to fill in detail on the face—care must be taken to avoid "red-eye" caused by flash in line with the lens being reflected back from the eyes. The darker the room, the more pronounced this effect will be, as the subject's pupils will become dilated. To avoid this, use the flash from an angle rather than in line with the lens axis, or bounce the light onto the subject from a reflector card. Bounced flash, although requiring more exposure due to the increased distance the light must travel, helps avoid the loss of form and texture that is evident with hard, direct lighting.

Because of the brief duration of electronic flash, it is difficult to judge what will happen when the light falls on the subject. In the studio an instant camera equipped with flash is often used to test exposure, but this is rarely possible with outdoor subjects. To calculate correct exposure for a photograph combining flash and daylight, work out the aperture setting for flash alone, based on the dis-

tance of the subject from the camera. Reduce the aperture half a stop or more to allow for the daylight. Then, with the aperture fixed, meter for a shutter speed to expose for the background. This ensures that the subject (the area covered by the flash) will not record too brightly in relation to the rest of the picture.

A simple method of calculating flash exposure is to use the guide number advised by the manufacturer of your flash unit for the rating of the film used. Divide the flash-to-subject distance into the appropriate guide number to determine the required f-stop. This applies both to feet and meters. For fast-moving subjects like the skateboarders shown above right, the exposure should be predetermined from your chosen position so that you are ready to shoot instantly.

The use of electronic flash to record movement is an effective technique in conditions that would otherwise preclude successful shooting, particularly in poor daylight where the use of a shutter speed fast enough to freeze the action would result in serious underexposure and loss of essential detail.

As correct exposure under these varying circumstances is difficult to calculate precisely, experience is the best guide. It is therefore worth practicing the technique in order to attain consistently good results.

The midair drama
(below) is enhanced by
the shadow caused by
flash, which helps to
separate the skate-
boarder from the back-
ground. Here the
shadow is a vital part
of the photograph, but
unwanted shadows
may spoil flash shots
unless care is taken to
avoid them.

Electronic flashguns have a calculator disc
enabling you to determine the aperture settings
required for various distances. You set the film
rating, turn the disc to the distance of the subject
from the light source and read off the correct
f-stop. The flash guide numbers are worked out
on the basis of the inverse square law. This is a
mathematical formula for establishing the
increase or decrease in the intensity of light falling
on a surface as the distance between the light
source and the surface alters. As the diagram
(right) shows, if distance from source is doubled,
the intensity of light on a surface is quartered.

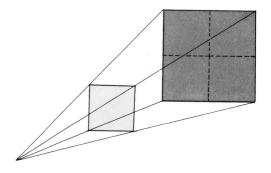

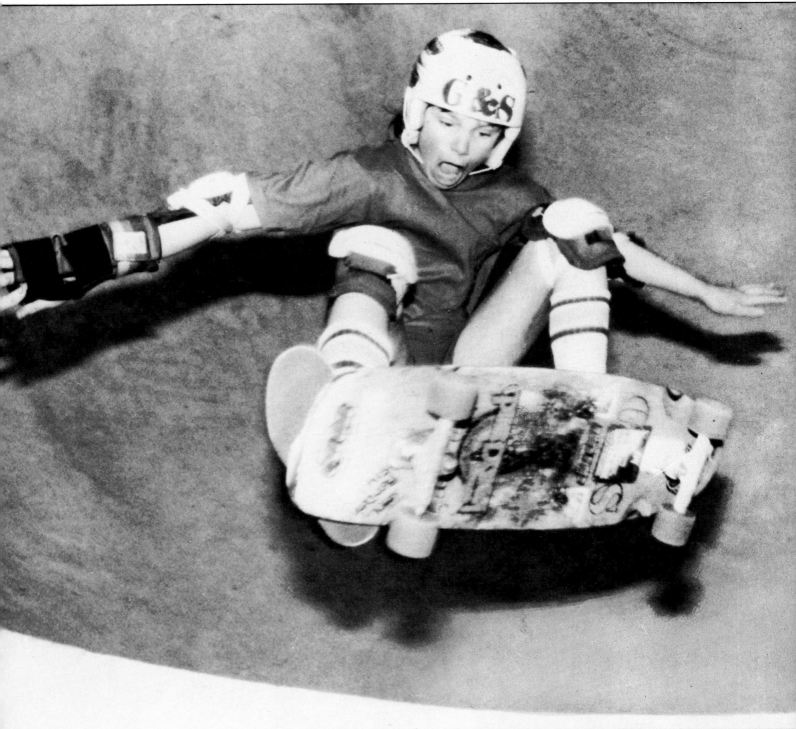

Memorable pictures of children can capture the atmosphere and excitement of thunderstorms, fog, rain and snow. Modern films are capable of recording many of the special light qualities characteristic of different types of weather, ranging from the intense color of storm clouds to the delicate tones of mist and the luminosity of snow.

A rainstorm has left the black tarmac wet. It reflects the sky and, therefore, seems light grey. Reflected light from water lying on a surface can often be exploited in this way to transform what would otherwise be an uninteresting background. Because the jacket is saturated, it has absorbed more light than when dry and so its color is strengthened. The wet hair, of course, also appears darker. *Minolta, 50 mm, 1/250, f5.6, Ektachrome 64.*

Bright, frosty morning light has vividly illuminated the bold colors of the girl's clothing, while capturing the subtle tones in her face and in the background. The vibrant red of the glove exaggerates the foreground while the blues of her other clothes appear to retreat. Blues and reds are beautifully blended in her chilled face, harmonizing with the intense colors of her garments. *Leicaflex, 90 mm, 1/250, f2.8, Ektachrome 64.*

Photographing in adverse conditions

A frosty morning is encapsulated in this picture of a young girl sucking an icicle. Her subtle skin-tone is clearly illuminated by the bright morning light and enhanced by the bold colors of her clothes against a cold blue background.

Contrary to popular belief, bright sunny conditions are not always the best for taking photographs—some of the most interesting pictures have been created in unusual weather conditions.

Children love snow and are happy to play in it for a long time, which gives the photographer ample time to catch a candid picture. They are also usually uninhibited in snow because of the exciting opportunities it offers. A snow scene can be delicate and picturesque or dramatic and full of leaden tones if taken in such heavily overcast conditions as just after a snowstorm. Essentially, a snow scene is a monochromatic situation, so the intense color of a child's clothing can give a picture considerable impact if balanced correctly against the background.

Photographers often have problems when taking an exposure reading of snow, so it is a good idea to bracket the exposure, taking one or two frames on each side of the "correct" exposure, half a stop apart. If using a hand-held meter, take a reflected light reading holding the meter close to the subject's face or, if the child is some distance away, use your own hand to avoid underexposure of the flesh tones.

Although uncomfortable, rain is useful to the photographer because it transforms colors and creates shiny surfaces on previously unexciting subjects. The possibility of spectacular results usually makes the effort of photographing in the rain worth while. If it begins to rain heavily, protect the camera with a plastic bag with a hole

for the lens and keep on a filter (preferably 81A) to prevent rain getting on the lens. With stormy skies, expose for the highlights to capture the dramatic background.

The atmospheric effects that are produced by mist and fog, which are often such attractive features of landscape photographs, can also contribute to successful photographs of children. In foggy and misty conditions, light is diffused by moisture in the air, producing very gentle modelling. Expose for the highlights if you want to record mist or fog—it can provide a useful background, blotting out or softening detail that might otherwise make the composition confused.

When travelling abroad you may encounter even more extreme weather and atmospheric conditions. Protect your camera and films from severe heat and cold, sand and dust and water (especially seawater).

Sand and dust are serious problems to cameras. They jam the mechanics, scratch the lens and wear the lens threads. Before going to an extremely dusty location, wrap the camera in a plastic bag with a hole for the lens and one for a hand. Seal with tape around the edges. Protect the lens with a filter. If any dust does get on the lens, do not attempt to wipe it off—blow it off with a puffer before cleaning with a lens tissue.

In a tropical environment, the enemy is moisture. High humidity encourages rust, which ruins the accuracy of the lens iris movements and shutter gear trains. Moisture also leads to the formation of molds both in the camera and on the film. Transparencies are extremely susceptible to moisture and should be stored in special containers. When not using them, keep your camera and films in sealed plastic bags with several packets of silica gel, then seal these hermetically in a camera case. The gel will need drying out from time to time by placing the packets in a warm oven.

In very hot countries, do not leave your camera unprotected in the sun because it may melt the cement holding the lens elements in place, causing permanent damage. If possible, keep the camera in a silver colored case to reflect the sun. Store film (exposed and unexposed) in a metal case with a thick polystyrene inner case and try not to open it in the heat of the day.

A quiet churchyard by the Thames caught my eye because of the interesting triangular shapes created by the dividing paths and the church itself. The threat of a summer storm in the evening sky, which I emphasized by using a red filter, provided a sharp counterpoint to the peaceful landscape with the two strolling youngsters.

A sudden snowstorm has transformed a bleak and forbidding Suffolk lane into a beautiful winter scene. The delicate tracery of the branches topped with snow form a vaulted arch into the distance. As the girl walks down the lane she is dwarfed by the trees and yet she forms the focus point, giving scale to the composition. To avoid flare from the bright foreground snow the exposure was based on an average meter reading from the shadow of the trees and the highlights of the snow.

131

The warm light of early morning and of evening provide exceptionally evocative atmospheres for photography. Relatively mundane objects often take on a new life and figures become integral parts of their settings. The reddish-orange haze subtly transforms colors and plays tricks with perspective. Sudden shafts of light can bring drama, contrasting brilliant color and shadow. It is worth getting up early or staying until dusk to catch not only the quality of light but also the sometimes unexpected activity of children before and after their daily routines.

The Moroccan children finishing a day's work were photographed a few seconds after the sun had set. They and the landscape are bathed in an afterglow, which has intensified the oranges and reds while creating an atmosphere of warmth and calm. The combination of evening light and the use of a long lens has flattened perspective so that the landscape behind the truck looks like a backcloth.
Pentax, 200 mm, 1/125, f5.6, Ektachrome 200.

The dramatic lighting on the Peruvian children returning home was caught by anticipating the precise moment the shaft of light would fall on their brilliant costumes. The striking contrast between intense color and the somber shadow of their forms is set against a strongly modelled landscape floating mysteriously in the background.
Pentax, 135 mm, 1/60, f5.6, Ektachrome 200.

The changes of natural light

The evening light in Morocco after sunset casts a warm yellow glow over the landscape. This diffuses the colors of the children's clothes and skin tones, and has the effect of subduing shadow areas and highlights alike.

The success of a great many photographs is governed by the light in which they are taken. In the studio or at home this can be dictated by the photographer using artificial light but in the open the photographer must depend on available natural light and be able to recognize its favorable qualities. Sometimes this will mean waiting for the appropriate time of day to get just the right lighting conditions.

The time of day has a great effect on the kind of light there is. In the morning, when the sun is near the horizon, red light is predominant because the blue waves are filtered out by dust particles suspended in the air.

If there is little cloud, dawn produces a pure light that is excellent for photography and certainly worth getting up for. Sunrise causes the light to "warm up", to gain more red tones. Speed is essential at this time because the light changes so quickly. As the sun rises through the morning the sunlight becomes brighter and less favorable, although until about 10 o'clock it is still clean and good and the shadows are sharply defined but not completely black.

Midday light is hard, less red and directly overhead. Although daylight color film is balanced to reproduce colors most accurately under mean noon daylight, on the whole it is not a good time for photography. When taking portraits the strong light creates ugly shadows under eyes, noses and chins and causes children to screw up their eyes. Avoid this time, if possible, or prevent these problems by using flash or a reflector to fill in the shadows. Better still, move your subject into partial shade and expose for the face, not for the sunny background.

In the late afternoon, the light again becomes more suitable; it is low, warm (which is very good for skin tones) and it casts long cross-lights over the landscape. On hot sunny days there may be a considerable haze in the background. Use an ultra-violet or 81A filter if you wish to penetrate it. The later it gets, the longer and more blue the shadows become. In mid-winter, of course, the afternoon is very short and the light fails rapidly.

Sunsets are often colorful and exciting as backgrounds but you need to be at the right spot to record them because the light changes rapidly. It is best to take a tripod because long exposures may be necessary.

Dusk can be a beautiful time; the light is diffused, the colors muted and there is a stillness which, if captured, can create tremendous atmosphere in a photograph.

Filters

The use of filters can appreciably improve a photograph in certain conditions; the sort of filter you use depends on whether you are taking black and white or color pictures. Special effects filters, which can be used with any film, are discussed on pages 146-7.

Filters used for black and white film lighten their own colors and those colors in the same area of the spectrum, and darken complementary colors. The effect is to increase the contrast on the negative. A yellow or orange filter darkens the tone in a blue sky and separates it from the clouds. A red filter turns blue sky almost black; the clouds remain white.

Filters for color photography (known as correction and conversion filters) change the color temperature of the light reaching the film by increasing their own colors and blocking out complementary colors. This is useful for balancing the color temperature of the light when it varies from that for which the film is made.

The 81 series of filters is good for improving skin tones; the 81B adds a rich, suntanned effect. Filters 1A and 2A add a pink tone.

Filters can either be glass discs or thin gelatin film. Glass ones last longer than gelatin but gelatin filters are cheaper. Treat your filters as carefully as your lenses: do not touch or wipe them except (with glass only) with a clean lens tissue.

Colored filters reduce the amount of light reaching the film so unless you have through-the-lens metering you must allow for this.

A bleak and menacing industrial landscape was matched by the dark stormy weather. To increase the contrast between the clouds and the sky, I used a yellow filter. The picture's horizontal lines are interrupted by the stiff vertical cooling stacks and chimneys. A feeling of movement is introduced in an otherwise static landscape by the homeward-bound schoolboy and emphasized by using a slow shutter speed, so that the figure of the boy is recorded as a slight blur.

A misty morning, with the sun breaking through provides the atmospheric conditions for this Thames-side cricket match. The overall light gives a diffused tonal range. The reflections of the power station link the background to the foreground. In this way, the environment is harmonized with the activity of the boys.

Organized sporting and physical activities provide firm disciplines for the exuberant energy of teenagers. Intense concentration on practicing skills excludes self-consciousness. This concentration and the frequent repetition of movements, particularly in the dance studio and gymnasium, provide the keen photographer with wonderful opportunities to record the grace and agility of adolescents.

Natural lighting conditions, even in interiors with obtrusive backgrounds or furniture, can be turned to advantage in capturing the true atmosphere of a situation. In this front-lit photograph of a rehearsal, I have used the way the light falls off to exaggerate the perspective and to emphasize the relationship of the four girls. *Pentax, 35 mm, 1/125, f5.6, Ektachrome 400.*

Backlighting in the ballet studio has provided a luminous background against which to show the elegance and lightness of the dancer. I took a reading by standing with my back to the window to get an approximate value for the area in which the girl was standing and then opened the aperture one more stop so as to give detail in the shadow area. *Pentax, 35 mm, 1/250, f8, Ektachrome 400.*

The effects of backlighting

Backlighting is one of the most effective ways of conveying a sense of lightness and grace in subjects as well as being wonderfully evocative of a sunlit atmosphere.

The results of backlighting are well worth the problems caused by the contrast between highlights and shadow areas. On cameras that have manual controls, or automatics with override, effects will differ greatly if exposed for highlight, for shadow, or for an average of the two. Automatic cameras without override respond to high-intensity light and can cause underexposure.

If photographing towards light, use a lens hood and avoid shooting straight into the sun. Strong sunlight passing directly through the lens causes secondary images (halation effect) or flaring (a diaphragm image, as in the photograph below). However, the sun masked behind clouds, trees or buildings can produce impressive effects.

The sunny atmosphere of this scene reinforces the pleasure and excitement the little girl shows at being swung down the steps by her parents. As well as conveying the impression of sun-filled space, backlighting has simplified the image, the steps reducing to a pattern of highlights and shadows.

The high spirits of these children enjoying a party in a beautiful summery garden are wonderfully conveyed in this photograph that includes their dancing shadows. Whichever way I photographed, this was a complicated subject. The most interesting picture I could find at ground level involved shooting against the light and using a wide-angle lens.

Long shadows indicate that the boy and cows (far left) were photographed in the evening, when backlighting has nearly reduced the shapes to silhouettes. The deliberate elimination of detail concentrates attention on the action.

The great contrast (left) of the glaring light behind and deep shadow in front has added a dynamic quality to the picture of a girl running. I have exposed to get some detail in the figure.

Rim-lighting can be very evocative of the fun and pleasure of outdoor living (below). The figures of children on a pole have been picked out against a cool, shady background.

The half-seen face of an adolescent girl, partially obscured by a veil, has produced a powerfully mysterious image. Despite the pattern of the mesh, the elegant structure of this girl's face is well defined. In order to give sufficient detail I have allowed for a half stop extra exposure over the light reading from the surface mesh. Any partially transparent material can be used to create interesting variations on more conventional portraits.
Leicaflex, 90 mm, 1/125, f8–f11, Ektachrome 64.

A telephone booth, bearing its crude message of love, is like a capsule enclosing the girl absorbed in her intimate conversation. The reflecting glass suggests an element of secrecy but allows us to see enough of the three-dimensional space to contrast with the bright red surface of the outside world.
Pentax, 50 mm, 1/125, f8, Ektachrome 64.

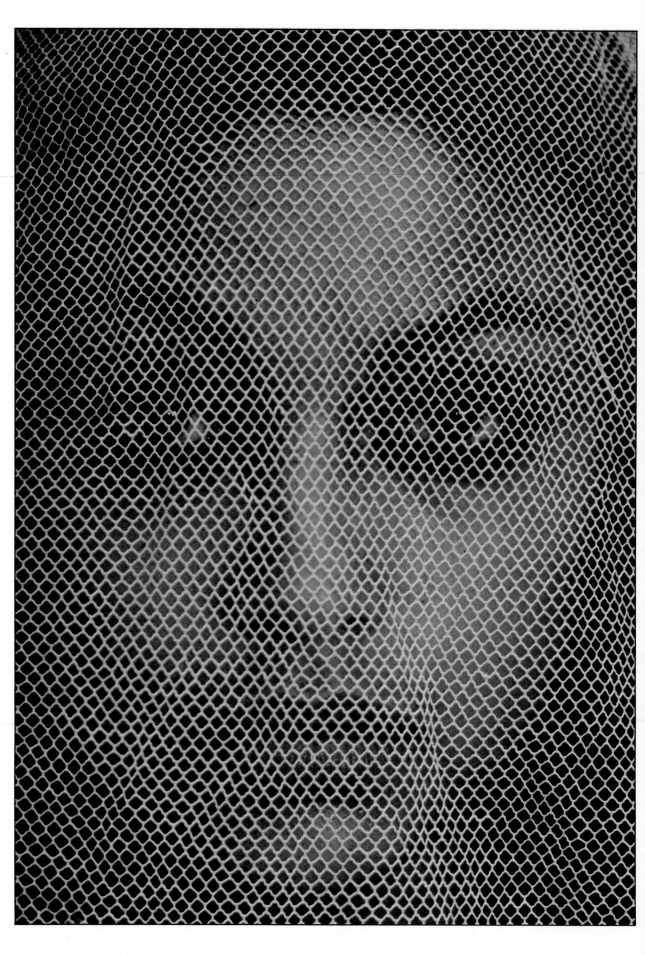

Reflections and distortions

Reflections on the window create an intimate atmosphere in which the girl feels unobserved. The glass also softens her image slightly and is a contrast to the hard red surrounding.

A great deal of the photographer's skill lies in being able to eliminate the problems of unwanted flare, reflection and lens distortion. Most modern cameras, with their coated lenses, fine optical glasses and filters, have been developed to minimize these difficulties. However, the creative photographer often uses these shortcomings to advantage, producing unusual effects and exciting photographs. Mirrors, water or any polished surface can reflect the image with varying degrees of distortion, and, when used imaginatively, enhance the subject.

Try using reflections when taking a formal portrait of a child. Set your subject either next to one mirror for a simultaneous front and side view, or between two mirrors at a right angle to each other for an infinity of reflections, a kaleidoscope of images. Experiment with different lighting techniques to make the result more dramatic.

When photographing a reflection in a shiny surface or in water, photograph the reflection and leave out the original. The image will be much softer and sometimes quite distorted so that you may not be able to identify the subject but you will have created a fantasy picture.

The fragmentary images between the subject and photographer caused by reflections on transparent surfaces can introduce an air of mystery. The young girl and her grandmother (below right) are not quite in our dimension; they are at once imprisoned and yet sheltered behind the window. The camera is almost intruding upon their privacy.

Photographing children through a window adds a touch of realism; it sets the scene. A window suggests that the children have not been posed or prettied and the spontaneity of the photograph is emphasized. The picture of the children seen through the car windshield (far right, bottom), is a vivid example.

A polarizing filter can be used to remove superfluous reflections but you may find that your photographs have lost some drama and interest in the process.

A penetrating study of the girl's wistful face is achieved when she is placed next to a mirror. Diffused light is provided from a window which, reflecting off the mirror, gently lightens the shadowed area.

An unguarded moment has been captured between a girl and her grandmother. Their closeness seems to be reinforced by the framework of the window and reflections on the panes prevent the intrusion of the onlooker.

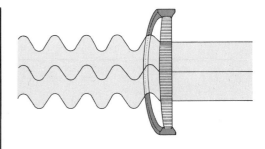

A polarizing filter blocks light reflected at an acute angle from a smooth, non-metallic surface such as polished glass, plastic or water. The filter is rotated until the reflected light disappears.

Minimizing reflections by using a polarizing filter (left) simplifies a picture but an image with the subject partially obscured by reflection can be more interesting.

These Singapore children were taken through the windshield of a slowly-moving car. The windshield does cause some distortion of image and color but the result is acceptable. It is preferable, though, to shoot through an open window for most photographs.

Dressing up and making up are partly fun, partly a serious matter of self-expression. Personal surroundings add to a portrait by reflecting current and often intense interests.
Leicaflex, 55 mm, 1/125, f6.3, Ektachrome 64.

The graffiti on the walls of a club room or the paraphernalia of a bedroom evocatively record teenage interests and exuberance.
Pentax 6x7, 105 mm, 1/125, f8, Ektachrome 200.

Dolly daydreams
Punk Rules O.K!
Mark is fat and smelly
'OW—THAT'S THE VERY LAST TIME YOU'RE CHANGING YOUR FILM THIS WAY !!
4789-62
11 am.
Taylor

Creating the atmosphere

The interests and pre-occupations of a teenage girl have been conveyed by framing her mirrored portrait with the clutter of her dressing table.

The emphasis in child photography is on capturing the reality of a situation: an expression, a gesture, an action related to a particular environment. The photographer usually attempts to record as faithfully as possible what he sees before him. But there are occasions when you will want to use your skills to enhance a mood, to create an atmosphere or feeling that is present largely in your own imagination. Such effects, though engineered rather than natural, can still look convincingly real in the final picture.

There are two ways of going about this. One is by the application of photographic technology in the form of filters, lenses, types of film, darkroom techniques and so on. The other is to rearrange the elements of the picture deliberately, to make the setting look the way you want it to look rather than the way it appears normally.

Wide-angle and telephoto lenses can be used, as we have seen, to change the normal optical vision of the eye. The grain of fast film can add texture, and use can be made of the individual color characteristics of different types of film. Filters are especially useful. Soft-focus or diffusion filters reduce the harshness and highlights of the image, giving a romantic, misty effect, which can also be achieved by lightly smearing petroleum jelly onto a glass filter. Fog filters have a similar effect, gently merging the colors and tones. Starburst filters can be used to dramatic effect to break up strong light into star-shaped flares. Try using one on such subjects as streetlights at night or the sun's reflection on water. Unlike most of the filters used for color correction, none of these special effects attachments requires a compensating exposure increase.

Try also the technique of panning to convey the excitement and vitality of action situations. Flash can also be used to freeze movement and suggest speed.

Even without using any specialist equipment, you can still modify images to suit your imagination. Careful composition can disguise the way a scene normally appears to the eye and alter its context. A corner of a vacant lot in the middle of a city can be made to look convincingly rural, or deliberate contrasting with the background can stress the essential character of a subject. The defiant stance of the girl opposite is emphasized by placing her in a staid, domestic setting which typifies the life-style she is rebelling against. Beware of making the overall effect seem too contrived: the elements of a picture should complement, not contradict, each other. Use special effects that are relevant, not for their own sake.

To capture or emphasize a particular atmosphere the use of filters is often necessary. A soft-focus filter diffuses highlights and reduces hard edges. Here the trees are softened so they do not overpower the couple, creating an impression of a romantic walk through a sunny glade. Use wide apertures; stopping the lens down will diminish the soft-focus effect.

An ultraviolet filter was partially smeared with petrolatum to frame two students. I chose this method rather than a soft-focus filter as I wanted to use a small aperture to get both students and background sharply defined.

Using a 250 mm lens from a distance enabled me to capture this moment of passion fairly close up. I included enough background to support the romantic mood, though the setting was, in fact, a vacant lot in the heart of a city.

A new dress is always an occasion for a photographic session. I wanted to underline the young girl's assertion of independence as it was expressed in her clothes and make-up. I consciously made a rather formal picture, placing her in contrast to her parents' pretentious suburban home.

The daredevil IMPS

Six or sixteen, the Imps have one thing in common—guts and determination to excel in the spectacular world of display riding

The wheels that make it all possible, and a very little Imp (left). The team on parade (below) show the precision and discipline that characterize their impressive display.

THREE YOUNG MASCOTS lead the way into the arena, signalling the start of forty minutes of skills and thrills performed by the Imps Motorcycle Display Team. The crowd marvels at the disciplined precision of the formation rides and pyramids; applauds the skill behind individual tricks; laughs at the comedy routines—and gasps as a gleaming motorcycle hurtles through a ring of fire or soars above a line of cars and bikes. It is a truly professional performance, yet the performers are all unpaid school-children between the ages of six and sixteen.

The Imps were formed in 1974 as part of a highly successful East London adventure scheme known as the Hackney Adventure Holiday Project. This independent voluntary organization was founded thirteen years ago by ex-military policeman Roy Pratt, a Senior Education Welfare Officer. In his professional capacity, he works to help juvenile offenders, providing a vital link between parents, schools, police and other agencies interested in the welfare of individual offenders.

Creative outlets

He was convinced that many of the problems he tackled daily sprang from the poor environment and deprived social conditions of East London. The Adventure Project was an attempt to provide country holidays and activities for local children, and to offer creative outlets for energies that might otherwise have been frustrated, with destructive results.

An early project involved the restoration of two elderly BSA Bantams, which were used to teach motorcycle riding. It was an immensely successful activity. In June 1974, five boys and an adult instructor performed at a Project Open Day in London to show parents that the activity was properly controlled. This first display went off so well that it was decided to form a team.

Through the following winter, a small group of boys worked hard in all weather learning to master their machines and put a small show together. The publicity that followed a press visit to the lonely Cotswold farm where they trained gave

the young riders a boost, and the team began to make a name for itself. By the end of 1976 the Imps had starred in numerous television programs and appeared all over the United Kingdom, thrilling millions of spectators who were astonished that such young people could work together to master the split-second timing, discipline and advanced riding skills that went into the spectacular display.

Isn't it dangerous?

Now the team travels all over Britain, and to Europe. A large transporter carries the motorcycles (supplied by Honda after the company's Japanese president saw a film called *Children of the World* that featured one of the Imps) and props, while an executive coach carries staff and riders. The team performs only at weekends and in school holidays and is always accompanied by voluntary adult staff—two instructors, three matrons to care for the children, two mechanics, a team engineer and the display commentator.

Roy Pratt explains how the team is recruited: "We have an open recruitment policy. Any youngster from the London Borough of Hackney may write (with parental permission) and ask to join. We then run a tough residential course in which the prospective members don't even see a motorcycle. The course involves communal living and very tough physical activity—we make no secret of the fact that it is designed to dissuade them from joining us, and this usually succeeds in reducing the numbers to the level needed to fill the vacancies caused by the retirement of senior team members at the ripe old age of sixteen. The new members are then put into serious training.

"We're often asked if the display is dangerous, but we believe that in order for young people to develop into responsible citizens, at some stage in their lives they need to take part in exciting activities. It is not possible to have adventure without some risk, but with training the risk can be reduced to an acceptable level.

The discipline and
enthusiasm that direct
the ebullient energy of
the boys of London's East
End (far left) who are
proud members of the
Imps team come from
ex-military policeman
Roy Pratt (right). The
program of training
he organizes and the
commitment he
demands produce
precision coordinated
teamwork capable of
such superb displays
as the mobile pyramid
(below left).

The daredevil
IMPS

"Many retiring team members continue to help the team on a voluntary basis. They pass on the benefit of their experience, and well over 70 per cent of the boys go on to find employment in the motorcycle industry. Their training, discipline and skill prove to be real assets in later life."

The success of the Imps may be judged by the fact that many members had very poor school attendance records before joining the team, preferring the streets to the classroom. This ceased to be a problem when they joined the team.

The spirit and objectives of the Imps Motorcycle Display Team are perhaps best illustrated by a fact that Roy Pratt relates with a pride that is tinged with sadness: "There are housing developments in this part of London where virtually all the children living there have some form of juvenile criminal record—all, that is, except the ones who have gone and joined a group such as ours. I think it is an indictment of our society that so many children get into trouble and go off the rails for want of a constructive outlet for their energy and drive."

Through the hoop for a fearless youngster (below). Whatever your point of view, the simultaneous shots of the display's climax (right) add up to a heart-stopping moment as the team's senior rider soars over two cars and ten bikes.

The daredevil
IMPS

Having become proficient at child photography, consider turning your skill to further advantage. There is steady demand from commercial picture agencies for good individual photographs of children, which they purchase outright or sell on your behalf. It is possible to sell complete series of pictures which tell a story. The local press and trade magazines are always on the lookout for good material, either single pictures or features. If the idea behind the feature is strong enough and the finished result of high technical quality with good visual impact, the top magazines would consider the material and—if it's good enough—publish it.

Even if you have no interest in selling work, there is satisfaction in creating a successful series of photographs, whether for exhibition purposes or to give the family album an added dimension. Whatever the objective, there are general rules that can be usefully applied to the creation of good feature material.

The idea

Find an idea that has a strong theme with suitable potential for varied photographs that complement and illustrate important ingredients of the story. There should be human interest and emotional appeal—humor, drama, achievement, triumph over the odds—or convey information that is new and interesting. Consider likely outlets and study them to get a feeling about the type of material they use. The local paper can serve as a good source of ideas with its coverage of news and forthcoming events. A brief news item often conceals a story worth following up in depth. The paper is unlikely to have a photographer at every noteworthy event. Children make excellent subject matter—they are naturally appealing and often become involved in activities that are in themselves full of interest.

Planning

Careful planning is essential. When the idea is formulated, consider how it may best be illustrated. This may mean shooting over a period of time. For example, you might decide to record preparations for Christmas at a children's home, starting two weeks before the big day and building up to that riotous party on Christmas afternoon. It may be necessary to obtain permission to shoot. Conditions may be difficult, requiring an assortment of film. Give some thought to the possibilities for unusual photographs—perhaps special effects—that will make the feature stand out. Very unconventional pictures, however, may have limited commercial value.

Shooting

Every picture should tell a story, but also fit into the planned series to enhance the whole. The photographs must have visual impact and variety, pace and cohesion. Some pictures should be quieter than others to vary the pace, and the camera technique should be changed to include the odd closeup or unexpected view. Take many variations of particular pictures to provide alternatives to choose from. Take portraits of individuals who are important. Work within the known limitations of your equipment—it is easy to get carried away and attempt the impossible, with predictable results. Other common mistakes include the production of a collection of photographs that do not form a natural series, having no coherent point, and a series which seems to consist of the same picture, in that lots of different people are shown doing the same thing. If the pictures are static, boring or repetitive the feature will not be a success.

The Imps

To illustrate the way in which a good feature may be created, I chose the Imps Motorcycle Display Team. The results appear on the previous pages. It was an ideal subject. That a team of children and young people between the ages of six and sixteen should be capable of a daring and apparently dangerous display of motorcycle acrobatics—performed to the highest professional standards—was itself surprising. But the thing that impressed me most was the way in which a bunch of East End kids who would otherwise have found destructive outlets for their energy had become disciplined and committed, channelling their energy in such a positive way. This served as the basis of the text—while the spectacular nature of the display provided ample scope for a series of exciting photographs.

Despite the widespread publicity received by the Imps, nobody had thought of doing a photo-feature. I visited the team, watched their program, discussed it with them and planned the series of photographs I wished to take. Weather conditions were far from perfect. Shooting took place on two separate days and I took as many variations on my chosen themes as possible to provide sufficient pictures of usable quality and to give a reasonable range of choice. The art directors of magazines and newspapers tend to look through the full selection—and immediately ask for the one picture that isn't there.

With the full cooperation of the team—who were prepared to repeat stunts until I was satisfied—I eventually obtained all the material I wanted. The feature was instantly used by a national newspaper.

Behind the glamour of display riding, there are hours spent acquiring a sound knowledge of how a motorbike works and maintaining equipment in immaculate condition.

Excitement and danger characterize the Imps in action—yet six years of displays have produced only one injury requiring hospital treatment. Superb discipline and months of dedicated training—channelling energies that might otherwise find a destructive outlet—go into this spectacular but safe display. It makes the ideal subject for a series of photographs with visual drama and a story to tell.

Index

Numbers in bold type refer to main entries in the book.

Acknowledgements

Art editor
Mel Petersen

Design assistant
Nigel O'Gorman

Technical consultant
Allan Shriver
Technical Editor
Amateur Photographer

Organizational researcher
Paddy Poynder

The author and publishers wish to thank the following people and organizations for their help in preparing this book:
Julia Hedgecoe, Kate Duffy, Toby Hogarth, Robbie Hunter of the G. & S. Skateboard Team, Tessa Marsh, Caroline Mazur, Roy Pratt and the Imps Motorcycle Display Team

ARTISTS: Harry Clow, Tony Graham, Kevin Maddison, Andrew Popkiewiez

RETOUCHER: Roy Flooks, O'Connor/Dowse

Italian Tourist Board, Jorge and Joe Koechlin Von Stein, Moroccan Tourist Board, Olympus Optical Co. (UK) Ltd., Pentax (UK) Ltd., Polaroid (UK) Ltd., Portuguese Tourist Board, Vivitar (UK) Ltd.